MW01075570

The Wilson Center, chartered by Cong
dent Woodrow Wilson, is the nation's key nonpartisan policy forum for
tackling global issues through independent research and open dialogue to
inform actionable ideas for Congress, the Administration, and the broader
policy community.

Conclusions or opinions expressed in Center publications and programs
are those of the authors and speakers and do not necessarily reflect the
views of the Center staff, fellows, trustees, advisory groups, or any individuals or organizations that provide financial support to the Center.

Please visit us online at www.wilsoncenter.org.

Jane Harman, Director, President, and CEO

For Michele

We know much more securely than we know almost any other social or economic factor relating to the future that, in the place of the steady and indeed steeply rising level of population which we have experienced for a great number of decades, we shall be faced in a very short time with a stationary or a declining level. The rate of decline is doubtful, but it is virtually certain that the changeover, compared with what we have been used to, will be substantial. . . . Nevertheless the idea of the future being different from the present is so repugnant to our conventional modes of thought and behavior that we, most of us, offer a great resistance to acting on it in practice.

—JOHN MAYNARD KEYNES, "SOME ECONOMIC CONSEQUENCES OF A DECLINING POPULATION," 1937

CONTENTS

ACKNOWLEDGMENTS

THIS BOOK WOULD NEVER HAVE BEEN WRITTEN without the support and encouragement of many people. I am grateful to the leadership of the Eisenhower School at the National Defense University for having granted me a sabbatical and generous travel support. The Woodrow Wilson International Center for Scholars provided a wonderful place for researching and writing. I thank them for choosing me as a Public Policy Scholar and allowing me to spend seven months in a scholar's paradise. There is no way I can fully express my appreciation to the many people on the Wilson Center's staff who assisted me.

My friend, Ambassador Pierre Buhler, an outstanding French diplomat and intellectual, played a significant role in launching me on this project through his article "Puissance et démographie, la nouvelle donne," which crystallized my interest. The Swedish deputy chief of mission, Karin Olofsdotter, assisted me in making appointments in Sweden, as did Robert Rhinehart. The distinguished demographer Gunnar Andersson of the Demography Unit of the Department of Sociology of Stockholm University, one of the intellectual centers for the study of population, set up a visit and discussion with his colleagues. I also met with Eskil Wadensjö, director of the Swedish Institute for Social Research. I was well received by several government ministries and organizations, including Tomas Pettersson and his colleagues at the Ministry of Finance, Lotta Persson at Statistics Sweden, Anders Ekholm of the Ministry of Health and Social Affairs, and Ambassador Olof Ehrenkrona of the Foreign Ministry.

Cyril Cosme of the French Embassy put together a fantastic program for me in France. The former director of the Institut national de démographie (INED), François Héran, spent a whole morning with me discussing French demography. Olivier Thévenon, also of the INED, shared his thinking with me, as did Julien Damon of Sciences Po, Jérôme Vignon and Isabelle Yeni of the Inspection générale des affaires sociales, and Bertrand Fragonard, president of the Haut conseil de la famille.

In Italy, I benefited from conversations with Raffaele Tangorra of the Ministry of Labor, Angelo Mari of the Department of Family Policy in the Office of the Prime Minister, Professor Alessandra De Rose of Rome University, and former minister the Honorable Giovanna Melandri. It was a great honor to meet with Senator Massimo Livi-Bacci, Italy's most famous demographer.

The Sasakawa Peace Foundation helped organize my trip to Japan. I would like to thank its executive director, Junko Chano, for her hospitality and Okamuro Mieko for planning my schedule. I learned much from meetings with Professor Wako Asato of Kyoto University, Dr. Takeo Ogawa of the Asian Aging Business Center, Hiroki Komazaki of the Florence Day Care Center, and the renowned demographers Naohiro Ogawa of Nihon University and Robert Retherford of the East-West Center, and from the candid observations of Kiyoko Ikegami, director of the Tokyo Office of the United Nations Population Fund.

In Singapore, I benefited from meeting Professor Saw Swee Hock of the Institute of Southeast Asia Studies, *Financial Times* bureau chief John Burton, Yap Mui Teng of the Institute of Policy Studies, and the director of the Prime Minister's National Population Secretariat, Quah Ley Hoon, who even took me around her neighborhood to help me understand urbanism in Singapore.

I am grateful to the many interns at the Wilson Center and the Eisenhower School who worked with me on this project. Two outstanding American demographers, Nick Eberstadt and Jack Goldstone, provided valuable guidance during this project. Many colleagues and friends read parts of the manuscript and offered valuable comments—including Irene Kyriakopoulos, Desaix Myers, Sonya Michel, Chris Barrett, and Anne Daguerre on France; Ambassador Roberto Toscano on Italy; Hsiao-Li Sun and Andre Laliberté on Singapore; and Karin Lang and Jordan Sand on Japan. Jim Anderson read the whole manuscript and provided important comments from the point of view of a scientist immersed in public policy. Shannon Brown helped me navigate Singapore's politics and society, traveled with me to Singapore and Japan, and read much of the manuscript. George Topic played a critical role in the development and revision of the book. His enthusiasm and perceptive critique of the penultimate draft incited me to fully develop my conclusions. Sonya Michel, one of the reviewers of the manuscript, provided valuable suggestions for revisions.

No one deserves more thanks than my wife, Michele Lamprakos —first, for making my life happy; and second, as the best editor and critic for whom anyone could hope.

A brief version of the main argument of this book appeared in the May–June 2012 issue of *Foreign Affairs*, with the title "Baby Gap: How to Boost Birthrates and Avoid Demographic Decline."

This book represents only the opinion of its author and should not be construed as reflecting the opinions of the National Defense University, the U.S. Department of Defense, or the U.S. government.

The Other Population Crisis

Introduction:
The Threat of Declining Birth Rates

THE DEMOGRAPHIC TRANSITION, which has been reordering the global population for two hundred years, consists of two phases. In the first—thanks to better nutrition, public health, and medicine—mortality rates decline and populations expand; in the second, birth rates adjust down. The first phase usually produces overpopulation. Overpopulation is something we know a lot about and fear. The "population bomb" revived the dark prophecies of Thomas Malthus. The population of the globe is still rising, threatening to strain resources and undermine the stability of many states.[1] But while overpopulation continues to plague the poorest continent, Africa, and much of the world's most troubled region, the Middle East, it has abated in most developed countries. Instead of overpopulation, we face a new demographic threat to national security: declining birth rates, and even declining populations. This threat is a direct result of the second phase of the demographic transition.

The implications of declining birth rates have just begun to fix our attention. The population of many European and Asian states is in absolute decline, or very soon will be. Nowhere in Europe do birth rates attain replacement levels, although a few countries come very close. The same is true for much of Asia, including Japan and South Korea. This population decline is new. In the past, populations declined temporarily as a result of natural causes, such as plagues (e.g., the Black Death) or wars and conflicts (wars and disease have often gone together). But until the nineteenth century, there was no precedent for a decline in birth rates on a national scale based on choice.

Sex and childbearing have become separate. Sex does not have to lead to procreation; having children is a matter of conscious decision-making. Increasing gender equality has challenged "traditional" forms of marriage and the family. With the advent of the welfare state, children are less necessary to support aging parents and are often perceived as an expense (economic and emotional) that many adults are hesitant to assume.

The question of low birth rates lies at the intersection of many of the great themes of human existence on both the personal and national levels: the meaning of life, at a time when sexuality has been separated from procreation; the reinterpretation of the role of children in a society when they are no longer an economic necessity; the tension between individual preferences for small families and the social need for replacement-level fertility; the impact on children of being brought up in nontraditional families or of spending less time with their parents and more in child care; the blessings and curses of longevity; and the relationship between population and power. This study would be incomplete if it ignored these themes, but it would also become unmanageable if it did not focus. Like Odysseus, we need to lash ourselves to the mast so that we can listen to the songs of the sirens without foundering on the reefs.

In this introduction, I first outline why there is a trend toward falling birth rates in the developed world, and why declining birth rates constitute a national security threat. Next, I discuss why the problem of low birth rates is often discounted and why the idea of state action meets with resistance. Then I present the low-fertility-trap hypothesis, which is followed by an explanation of why action needs to be taken sooner rather than later. Finally, the rationale is presented for the choice of case studies in this book.

The Decline of Birth Rates

The demographic transition began in the nineteenth century. Mortality rates fell, thanks to improvements in public health, medicine, and diet. Birth rates declined based on the decision of families to restrict pregnancy, but typically this did not take place immediately. France, the first country to experience the decline in birth rates, was also the first to achieve zero population growth: Because birth rates closely mirrored mortality, the population remained roughly stable. In Britain, there was a lag resulting in a "demographic dividend"— the large working-age population made rapid economic growth possible. Excess population (presumably those who could not expect to find land, jobs, or dowries) emigrated, much of it to the expanding empire, increasing national power. In Germany, increased population also contributed to the Industrial Revolution. Other countries, including Sweden and Italy, produced similar waves of emigration. In unhappy Ireland, Malthusian prophecies played out, as emigration or starvation were the stark alternatives for many of the poor. For most societies, the first phase of the demographic transition was characterized by large families; this was not the case before the demographic transition nor the case after birth rates had adjusted down in the second phase of the demographic transition.[2]

The changing role of the family also led to a decline in the birth rate. In a seminal article published in 1937, the demographer Kingsley Davis explained that in premodern Europe, the family was the basic economic unit. Moreover, life was organized around kinship: "In so far as people need a 'cause' to live for, they can find it in the family, its extension back in time through ancestors and forward through progeny constituting the abstract principle around which concrete sentiments are clustered."[3] Davis pointed out that as Europe moved from a primarily agricultural society to a largely urban, industrial society, the family was no longer the unit of production and thus its economic role diminished. On the land, where the family retained more of its economic importance, having too many children became as much a problem as having too few. When the French Revolution gave peasants the land, these small plots could not be subdivided further.

For the urban middle and lower middle classes, which still thought in terms of family identity and sought social mobility, children became the vehicle of upward social mobility, a social ascent that was now possible in a more fluid society. In the nineteenth century, every bourgeois or middle-class family was like a general headquarters engaged in planning and executing a campaign of social promotion for their progeny (think of Jane Austen's novels). The instruments were education, work, and marriage. Sons required money for education, and daughters for dowries. Only sons could advance the family, however, because they carried on the family name. Resources needed to be concentrated on sons; therefore, social mobility required limiting the number of progeny. Family logic was supposed to trump (and often trampled on) individual desires; one of the great themes of modern literature was the conflict between the two—love marriage versus *mariage de raison*. In order to limit the number of progeny, contraception replaced delaying the age of marriage and celibacy, which had typified early periods. Contraception came to be used not just by a small elite, but increasingly by the middle classes and even the peasantry. The most common form was coitus interruptus, later to be supplemented by condoms and barrier methods of female contraception (and of course, if these failed, there was the possibility of recourse to abortion and abandonment).

Even with these less-than-infallible means of contraception (which limited both sexual pleasure and conception), the birth rate hovered around replacement level in France in the late nineteenth and early twentieth centuries. Other countries, including Sweden, also began to experience low birth rates, especially in the 1930s. Fears of declining birth rates emerged, and pronatalism arose as a movement, usually tied to the political right. The right tended to focus on the interests of the nation (as it saw them) as opposed to the interests of the individual; it attributed population decline to a growing emphasis on individual freedom and modernism. Pronatalism's rival, neo-Malthusianism, argued that social progress could only be made by reducing the population, especially that of the working class, in order to raise wages. Both presupposed the model of the limited state that would not provide social benefits to the disadvantaged.

The first states to engage in active pronatalist programs were the fascist states, motivated by fear of low birth rates (if not always the reality). For fascism, a growing population was tied to national power and vitality. Because German population policy was based on extreme racialism, Nazi goals included increasing the birth rate of Aryans while eliminating undesirables, with genocide an acceptable method. The experience of fascism or militarism made postwar Italy and Germany very reluctant to engage in population policy. Democratic states such as France and Sweden also initiated pronatalist programs before World War II; but because they were not afflicted by a bad conscience, they continued them after the war.

For a brief period after World War II, the problem of low birth rates seemed to have disappeared as the developed world experienced an unexpected baby boom, on a scale and duration far greater than that after World War I. But subsequently, and just as unexpectedly, birth rates fell, often to unprecedentedly low levels. At the root of this decline were several important factors, described as the "second demographic transition" by some (Lesthaege) but considered by others as merely a "more advanced state" of the demographic transition (Reher).[4] This period is characterized by several changes:

- The development of the birth control pill, which for the first time in history made it possible to fully experience sexual pleasure without the risk of pregnancy. The pill reduced birth rates because there were fewer "unplanned" pregnancies.

- The rise of the welfare state provided a social safety net for old age, reducing or eliminating the need for children as an economic support for parents. The cost of raising children rose, especially because education occurred over an extended time. Children, in short, became an economic liability to their parents.

- A declining role for children, as human fulfillment was increasingly seen in terms of individual self-realization rather than family mobility. The family unit, which had lost much of its economic role, also lost some of its affective significance. It was no longer true that one's station in life depended on whether one had children.

- A fundamental change in the life of women, who devoted only 14 percent of their adult life to childbearing and child rearing, as opposed to 70 percent in 1800, because of lower fertility and a longer life span.[5]

- The weakening of the "traditional family" by a vast increase in female participation in the labor force, the women's revolution, the rise of divorce, and the increases of non-traditional family arrangements like cohabitation. Already in 1937, Kingsley Davis raised the question of whether there was a fundamental incompatibility between the family and present-day society, as the family lost its economic and social purpose. It may still be too early to say. The family seems to survive as a fundamental social unit only by transforming itself. But by embracing many non-traditional arrangements, it sometimes comes to embody the very antithesis of the family that social conservatives are struggling to preserve.

An unrelated political development also had significant demographic consequences. As a result of the collapse of the Soviet Union and the Soviet Bloc, fairly successful pronatalist programs in Eastern Europe were eliminated as legacies of communist rule. This was probably a factor in the veritable collapse of birth rates.[6] In Russia and Ukraine, alcoholism, drugs, and HIV also resulted in dramatically higher mortality rates.[7]

The result of these profound demographic changes is a birth rate so low that it calls into question the very survival of many nations. The preference of individuals for few or no children is at odds with the national requirement to maintain a stable population.

Low Birth Rates as a National Security Problem

Why, it may be asked, are declining birth rates a problem? Declining birth rates constitute a problem for the survival and security of nations (in the broadest existential sense of national security) on at least four levels.

First, there is a change in the composition of the population in advanced societies from many young and working-age people and few seniors to one with few children, fewer people of working age, and many old people. Declining birth rates correspond with another important demographic trend, the great increase in life expectancy in developed nations. Increased life expectancy resulted from progress in sanitation, nutrition, and medicine. But longevity has an unfavorable impact on what is called the dependency ratio, or the percentage of working-age adults compared with nonactive citizens. The decline of this ratio has put great stress on the social welfare system. Fewer young people enter the workforce; longer education and training means that they enter later. Replacement-level birth rates mitigate the dependency ratio; lower birth rates exacerbate it. The American Social Security and Medicare programs are already at risk, despite replacement-level birth rates and significant immigration flows. The situation is obviously worse where neither replacement birth rates nor immigration cushions the impact of aging populations. The welfare state, as we shall see, has helped to stabilize birth rates in some countries. But low birth rates threaten the survival of the welfare state in others. A smaller number of working-age people will need to care for a mushrooming population of seniors.

Low birth rates are a national security threat in a second way, one that is harder to assess. For several hundred years, economic growth has been tied to prosperity. Growth in population has increased the size of the domestic market and labor force. The demographic "bonus" has often been a key factor in economic take-off. What would be the implications, on the contrary, of an absolute decline in population? That problem has not really been adequately studied, yet the populations of some countries, including Japan, are actually declining in absolute terms. Young people tend to be in the vanguard of technological innovation and new ideas. It would seem that a society with fewer young people would pay a huge price economically. Conceivably, the change in age distribution could lead to a form of gerontocracy, in which aging voters vote down policies favorable to children and families.[8] This would be no country for young men and women, that is, no place for change, new ideas, and innovation. We are moving into uncharted waters.

The third challenge to national security lies in changes in global population composition. In the eighteenth century, 20 percent of the world population lived in Europe. In 1913, 33 percent of the world population lived in Europe, the United States, and Canada. This proportion is estimated to shrink to 12 percent by 2050![9] Although rapidly expanding populations in less developed societies are hardly a source of strength (the demographic dividend is not much of a dividend if there is little or no economic development to absorb the growing population), the rise of great powers has tended to correlate with population increase. What are the consequences of population decline? Do Russian leaders suffer from insomnia as they ponder the empty borderlands along the border with China? Can rich but aging societies survive in a world in which they constitute a small and declining percentage of total world population, resembling gated communities for the rich and aging? How will population change affect the balance of power in the world?

The fourth national security challenge is immigration. Can population decline be remedied by immigration? In practice, immigration has served and is serving that purpose. But immigration never occurs without problems. No country has ever wholeheartedly extended a welcoming hand to immigrants. At worst, immigration provokes nativism, xenophobia, and racism (especially in times of economic crisis), even in countries that have greatly benefited from it, like the United States and France. How many immigrants can a society absorb? The threat of terrorism in the subcultures of alienated immigrants has become an obsessive concern. Multiculturalism is now under attack all over Europe. In the United States, ethnic ghettos tend to disappear as a result of social mobility. Elsewhere, large ghettos develop with several generations of immigrants and their children, either as a result of newcomers' reluctance to integrate into the host society or more often the reluctance of that society to integrate them.

Today, the global population is not shrinking, but a certain number of nation-states are. How will they respond? Some will argue that this is a false problem, that the nation-state is a phenomenon of modern times, the source of more harm than good, while the disappearance of the nation-state and its social/cultural identity would be a positive development. Not everyone would agree. Would Italians and Germans cheerfully welcome the end of Italy and Germany? And if the nation-state were to disappear, would not its successor still face the problem of declining population?

Even if the nation-states of Europe gave way to a strengthened European Union—which is increasingly doubtful—and European identity supplants national identity, the problem is not solved. The European Union as a whole suffers from the same problem of below-replacement birth rates as its component member states. Some would then argue that there is no need to increase European birth rates, because there are large numbers of potential immigrants from the developing world, many of them literally knocking at the doors of Europe today. A new global demographic balance could presumably be achieved by large-scale population migrations. But identities are shaped by culture and place. Human beings are not fungible. Not everyone will want to leave home for economic reasons, nor will large-scale migrations necessarily be welcomed. In the past, large-scale migrations were often tied to war and conquest. Will that be the case in the future?

There are many who claim that because of their high birth rates, Muslims will take over Europe, and that their birth rate is really a political tool (presumably the work of unidentified Elders of Islam). As often happens, the facts get in the way of this grandiose conspiracy theory. Immigrant birth rates rapidly fall to the national average. Thus, immigration may be neither an awful geostrategic menace, nor a solution to the problem of low birth rates (unless one posits indefinite immigration on a large scale).

Why the Problem of Low Birth Rates Tends to Be Ignored

Before proceeding, we need to confront an apparent paradox. Although there is a clear trend toward low birth rates throughout the developed world and this trend constitutes an important threat to national security, it has received relatively little attention. There are many reasons why its significance has been discounted and why the idea of state action to counter or mitigate declining birth rates meets with resistance. No policy to raise birth rates will succeed without taking into account the reasons for such resistance.

The overwhelming demographic concern for almost a century has been fear of overpopulation. That fear has been engrained in popular consciousness. There is no longer a generalized trend toward overpopulation in the developing world; birth rates have declined in many countries through the rise of contraception. Nevertheless, birth rates are exceedingly high in the Middle East, contributing to scarcity and political instability. Sub-Saharan Africa also manifests dangerously high birth rates. For many people, the real issue remains the "population bomb." It is therefore hard for much of the general public—who, after all, are also voters—to understand how low birth rates can be a problem for some countries, especially their own, while talk of overpopulation still dominates the news.

At the same time, the abuses, crimes, and depredations committed in the name of population control; the mass sterilizations, voluntary and otherwise; the belief that population control was an instrument of colonial or neocolonial control directed against the people of color of the developing world; and the dark history of eugenic thought and practice all contribute to suspicion or outright opposition to any form of "population policy." This legacy has also created skepticism concerning demographic "science," that is, doubt as to whether there is a genuine problem of low birth rates that needs to be "solved."

Of course, crimes have also been committed in the name of pronatalism. National leaders in Europe were raising the hue and cry over the dangers of depopulation in the 1930s. Fascists and Nazis pioneered pronatalist programs to counter perceived threats of population decline; Nazi pronatalist goals were linked with eugenic policies aimed at "purifying the race," which justified persecution of Jews, gays, Roma, and indeed everyone who was not an "Aryan." In countries where fascism never gained traction, like Sweden, there were eugenics policies that encouraged sterilization of "undesirables." Even the stalwart liberal Supreme Court justice Oliver Wendell Holmes Jr. declared that "three generations of idiots is enough" in voting to validate Virginia's compulsory sterilization law for the mentally retarded in *Buck v. Bell* in 1927. It is understandable that some will draw the conclusion to never again allow the state to interfere in the private life of the family. In any case, in Germany, Italy, and Japan, where fascist/militarist regimes practiced population policies, there has been strong resistance to pronatalist policies by the state.

The Catholic Church is an exogenous factor with much influence. It has raised its voice on this issue as well, but from a different point of view. In general, the Church opposes state involvement in the realm of the family, but not because it wants to defend the right to privacy. During the last two centuries, the Church has struggled against secularizing forces (and secularizing states) to retain power over the family and education. The Catholic Church did not oppose fascism per se, but fought its claims to authority in traditional areas of Church control. (Mussolini's Lateran Treaty of 1929 traded recognition of the fascist state for guarantees of Church autonomy.) After the collapse of fascism, the Church pushed back to regain as much control as possible over the family.

The Church never considered sexuality as a good per se, nor did it advocate pronatalism. Celibacy was the highest calling. But because this was considered to be beyond the capacity of the many, they were instructed to restrict sexual activity to marriage and to limit the sexual act to procreation. This became an increasingly central theme in the twentieth century, as contraception, abortion, and divorce became generalized. The Church is less and less able to influence the sexual behavior of its members but remains a powerful political force. Surprisingly, the way that the Church has chosen to defend the "traditional" family—for example, by opposing public child care—leads to lower birth rates, as we shall see.

Another factor undermining the prospect for pronatalist policies is that today's low–birth rate nations were often yesterday's countries with high birth rates. It is difficult to convince political leaders or the public to increase the birth rate in a country that, within recorded memory, needed to export its citizens to foreign climes (and in a time of recession and crisis may be doing so again), such as Ireland, Spain, and Italy. The feeling that a country has a high birth rate seems to persist long after it no longer has one—and continues to affect behavior.

Attempting to implement pronatalist policies is harder than engaging in population control. The Singapore government only a few decades ago, for example, decided to embark on population control. It probably did so at just the time that birth rates would have declined anyway. Birth rates did go down. Unfortunately, they continued to fall well below replacement levels. As we shall see, even a vigorous pronatalist policy was unable to reverse the trend. You can sterilize people so that they cannot procreate, but even the Nazis could not force people to breed.

There is a widespread belief that there exists some kind of natural law that regulates population, a little bit like the self-regulating Newtonian universe—or perhaps more like the economic world envisioned by free market theorists. The economic universe is not like a perfect clock; prosperity, after all, is punctuated by economic slumps, periods of inflation, and so on. But at least some neoliberal economists argue that if left alone, invisible hands will regulate it, and that government meddling interferes with its innate harmony. Similarly, it could be argued that declines in birth rates to extremely low levels would eventually right themselves and an equilibrium would be achieved at around replacement level. Many demographers expected that this would occur, but it has not happened. Assuming that the lowest low birth rates (total fertility rates below 1.5) continue in advanced societies for a generation or two, it would take extremely high birth rates to return to the previous population level, because the total population would have already greatly declined. Population does not seem to be self-regulating.

A somewhat different version of the self-regulating demographic universe is an incomprehensible universe. Demographic changes could occur in a way that is beyond our understanding. A good example was the baby boom. It would have been easy to predict a limited baby boom after World War II with soldiers coming home and families reunited. There was a small baby boom after World War I, for example. But that the baby boom would last for two decades was a complete surprise. And then, once everyone was accustomed to high birth rates and expected them to continue, they unexpectedly declined. For demographers, perhaps, as for historians, the owl of Minerva only sets sail after the sunset. It can be argued that if we cannot predict demographic trends, we should not engage in demographic policies. It is also possible that there will be yet another phase to the demographic transition of which we are not yet aware.

Another argument, very commonly encountered, is that pronatalist policies are ineffective. Many authors flatly state that pronatalist policies do not work.[10] If true, it would be the most powerful rationale for not engaging in what must necessarily be an expensive and futile endeavor. But the assertion is often made by fiat. Clearly, there are many cases where specific policies do not work. But that does not mean that no policies work. Some argue that birth rates can only be raised a small amount, about 0.2 percent. Even that may not be as inconsequential as it seems at first blush. And the case studies presented in this work demonstrate that, at a minimum, some policies do work in specific situations. It is also clear that an abrupt termination of pronatalist policies led to a rapid decline in birth rates in Eastern Europe.

An increasingly common argument against pronatalism is environmental. Why should we decry the prospects of a declining population in advanced societies? Overpopulation has damaged the ecosystem, undermined biodiversity, and brought on climate change. The agricultural advances used to feed the human population have terrible side effects. A lower population would be in the interest of the planet. There is real validity to this argument. The problem is that it fails to take into account the imbalance of population trends. Lower birth rates in the developing world would be to its advantage; lower birth rates in the developed world would be to its detriment. The goal of a sustainable global population may require convergence of the developed and developing world to a common level that presumably would be a global replacement-level population. Of course, this presupposes that climate change does not make it impossible to sustain the current level of the global population or the increased total populations predicted by 2050, which may not be a safe assumption.

One reason that nations may fail to respond to the birth rate problem, even though they are conscious of it, is that as society ages, more and more political power accrues to the old. It might seem that no one should be more conscious of the need to ensure a broad tax base than the old. But that assumes a sense of enlightened self-interest in which the elderly envision effects beyond their own generation. At a time of strained public budgets, expenditures may seem to be part of a zero-sum game. Money spent for mothers and children would constitute money not spent on seniors, and therefore seniors will not hear of it. In that sense, there is a dynamic that could lead aging societies to age further. In some places there seems to be an active dislike of children on the part of seniors who hole themselves up in communities where children are unwelcome.

Perhaps the most important reason why the problem of low birth rates may not be readily susceptible to policy solutions is that because of the incremental nature of population decline, there is never a "population crisis." Wars break out on a specific date in a specific place, and nations must react promptly and fully. An earthquake, a pandemic, or a tsunami strikes and immediate action is called for. The global financial and economic crisis of 2008–9 manifested itself in a matter of weeks and demanded a rapid policy response. But even if birth rates are intolerably low, there is never a crisis. Every day, every month, every year the population declines in some countries, but the decline is always incremental. Politicians rarely respond well to long-term, incremental problems no matter how important, because they rarely think in a long-term way. Most of the time, such issues will be put off indefinitely, unless there are powerful interest groups that demand action. This is especially true if dealing with such an issue requires a large commitment of resources, financial and otherwise. Low birth rates considered alone are therefore unlikely to arouse the passion and commitment required for important public policy initiatives. But important policy initiatives may be possible when demographical concerns are seen as an indispensable part of the solution to a larger national crisis.

And finally, there is the incredible human capacity for denial. Consider climate change. The scientific evidence in favor of climate change is more or less clear: The consequences are dire. The impact of climate change is already being felt. Yet the willingness of states and the international community to face up to this problem and act effectively is lacking. Worse still, many deny the reality of climate change, and the issue has become politicized.

The obstacles to recognition of the dangers posed by declining birth rates are thus considerable. The low-fertility-trap hypothesis to which we now turn explains the dangers of inaction.

The Low Fertility Hypothesis

The fact that there are no invisible hands that stabilize fertility at something near the replacement level—contrary to earlier expectations—but that, on the contrary, nothing prevents continued decline, is the basis for serious concern about the demographic future in developed societies. But the situation may be even worse. What if once fertility decline continues for an extended period, there are mechanisms that create a self-reinforcing downward spiral? In several important papers, demographer Wolfgang Lutz develops the concept of a "low fertility trap."

This trap consists of three independent but mutually reinforcing components, which he calls demographic, sociological, and economic. The demographic element is based on the fact that under conditions of declining birth rates, the age distribution of a population changes. "If there are fewer births today, there will be fewer potential mothers down the road, which in turn will bring the number of births further down."[11] The sociological component presupposes that the decline in birth rates will affect the number of children desired by parents. Living in a world of small families and only children will eventually make future parents likely to have fewer children. All pronatalist policy is founded on the effort to reduce the gap between desired number of children and actual number of births. If the desired number of births falls below replacement level, it is hard to imagine how any policy can work. And that has already occurred in Germany and Austria.

The third component is based on the idea that people will marry and have children if they have an optimistic outlook toward the future—that is, the relationship of their aspirations vis-à-vis their expectations (the standard of life they were accustomed to versus their expected standard of living). This can be represented by the ratio of their income divided by their father's income. In the case of four countries that belong to the Organization for Economic Cooperation and Development (Italy, the United Kingdom, Sweden, and Japan), since the 1970s this ratio has shown continuous decline. What we are facing, in other words, is the decline of the kind of social mobility that instilled optimism in developed societies after World War II, which in turn will lower the propensity to have children.

Lutz draws the following conclusion from his analysis:

> But there is an even more immediate political dimension which may add some urgency to the question of whether governments should get actively involved in trying to raise the level of period fertility. Should the dynamic and self-reinforcing mechanisms assumed to be at work under this hypothesis indeed become a dominating force in determining the future level of fertility, then

possible action to counteract this trend will have a far greater chance of succeeding if it is implemented soon. Once the assumed demographic regime change is far enough advanced, it may be very difficult, if not impossible, to reverse. Once the ideal family size of the young generation has begun to decline and fall well below replacement, as seems to be happening currently in the German-speaking countries, then it may be too late for a reversal of this trend. In this respect, particularly the Central and Eastern European countries that used to have fertility not so far from replacement level until the transition around 1990, and still have high family size ideals today despite a precipitous decline in period fertility, seem to be in a critical stage that might still be influenced by policies. If period fertility in these countries should increase in the near future—possibly through policies affecting the tempo of fertility rather than cohort fertility—this may still help to stop the "tanker" of changing family size norms from making a full turn. Through such immediate action, an irreversible demographic regime change might still be stopped by making children a part of a normal life again. This will enhance the chance that in the future, young people will have their norms shaped in such a way that they still see children as part of the life they wish to live, as seems to be the case in France and the Nordic countries. A similar chance may still exist in the Mediterranean countries, where fertility declined long ago, but the ideals still seem to be rather high on average, at least up to 2001.[12]

Whether or not government policy enables nations to escape the low fertility trap may be the decisive factor in determining their demographic future.

The Structure of This Book

This book is based on the assumption that attempting to achieve a replacement-level birth rate is a valid goal of government policy. It examines five national case studies in Europe and Asia to ascertain what factors encourage or discourage maintaining a birth rate that is close to replacement, whether state policies can make a difference, and, if so, under what circumstances. The case studies represent countries from different geographical regions and varying policy approaches. Two have been successful in stemming population decline, and three have been unsuccessful. The cases are Sweden, France, Italy, Japan, and Singapore.

As delineated in chapter 1, Sweden faced low birth rates in the 1930s. Gunnar Myrdal and Alva Myrdal, who helped develop economic policies to free Sweden from the Great Depression, developed a new approach to demography and transformed pronatalism from a conservative policy to a left-wing program based on gender equality. Their ideas were then incorporated into the Swedish model of the welfare state. Swedish Social Democracy became the first party of the left to make pronatalism a key element of its program. The chapter describes the influence of Myrdal on Swedish policy, the evolution of that policy and the reasons for its relative success. Swedish policy has been distinguished by its clarity, simplicity, and commitment to gender equality, making it possible for women to reconcile work and children.

France, as described in chapter 2, was the first country to undergo the demographic transition. Birth rates in the late nineteenth and early twentieth centuries were very low, and in many years deaths exceeded births. French concerns about birth rates were founded on national security concerns; France experienced fears of national decline after defeat by Prussia in 1871, which some attributed to a low French birth rate. But France was unable to achieve successful pronatalist policies until the development of an activist state with high social welfare spending. The chapter shows how after the 1960s, French policy, initially familialist, came to focus on gender equality and reconciliation of work and family. Unlike Sweden, France today has a nearly replacement-level birth rate. France is a big country; it cannot be argued that its policy success is due to the homogeneity of its population or its small size.

If Sweden and France represent two successful models for improving and maintaining moderately high birth rates, Italy, conversely, as examined in chapter 3, is a study in failure: It has extremely low birth rates, an aging and absolutely declining native population, and a signal inability to develop policy. The reasons for this failure lie in the symbiosis of familialism and ineffective government, both of which are analyzed in the chapter. Italy's problems are similar to those of much of Mediterranean Europe.

Japan is an important case study in and of itself, as shown in chapter 4. It was one of the great postwar success stories, rising to become the world's second-largest economy. Yet in the last two decades, Japan has become mired in economic and demographic stagnation. It is now demographically the world's oldest nation, and its birth rate one of the lowest. Japanese population policy has been ineffective. At the same time, Japan refuses to consider opening itself to immigration. Its inability to counteract declining birth rates is tied to its failure to restore economic growth. Why has Japan been unable to find a way out of this crisis?

Since Singapore gained its independence, its government has never hesitated to intervene in demographic policy. As described in chapter 5, in the 1960s it acted vigorously and successfully to encourage birth control to make itself into a modern and advanced nation. It then initiated a eugenics policy. Finally, as birth rates fell to levels well below replacement, it tried unsuccessfully to stimulate higher birth rates. On the other side of the policy equation, encouragement of large-scale immigration has backfired politically, leading to unprecedented losses by the ruling party in the 2011 parliamentary elections. Although Singapore has been willing to employ social engineering to deal with its demographic policies, it has not succeeded.

In the conclusion, I argue that demographic forces are leading to a decline of birth rates in almost all developed and many developing societies. Without government intervention, birth rates tend to fall below replacement level. The examples of France and Sweden show that properly conceived family policies can counteract or at least mitigate this trend. France and Sweden succeeded by devoting significant financial resources to family policy and supporting women's need to reconcile work and children. The success of a similar approach in other countries depends on two main factors: first, whether adequate national resources can be allocated, despite the decline of the welfare state; and second, whether the implications of gender equality will be accepted by political leaders and the population.

CHAPTER ONE

Swedish Population Policy: The Pronatalism of the Left

I N A 2002 ARTICLE, "Gender Equality: A Key to Our Future?" Lena Sommestad, a women's historian and then Social Democratic minister of the environment, explained why Sweden's "gender equality policies built on a strong tradition of pronatalist and supportive social policies" were relevant to a Europe faced with declining birth rates and aging populations. According to her, Sweden's combination of pronatalism and feminism accounted for the success of Swedish pronatalist policies. She urged feminists elsewhere to overcome suspicion of pronatalism. By enabling women to both work and have children, Sweden maintained high birth rates, unlike countries that supported traditional views of women's roles. Extensive state intervention was needed to support families with children. Noting that "women's access to the labor market appears to be a prerequisite for higher birth rates," she observed that Sweden gives no benefits to women as wives, but only as workers. She argued that "countries that do not stigmatize non-marital cohabitation have a better chance of maintaining higher fertility rates. Since there is a decline in the marriage rate all over the industrialized world with later and fewer marriages and more divorces, non-marital births are needed to compensate." Sommestad attributed the origins of Sweden's population policies to Gunnar and Alva Myrdal's work in the 1930s.[1]

Sweden constitutes the paradigm of a society based on egalitarian, social democratic, and pronatalist policies, and a radical view of the family. Sweden made a series of clear and logically consistent choices. It led the way to the creation and development of the modern welfare state with unequaled determination, consistency, and coherence. In this chapter, the origins and characteristics of Sweden's approach to population policy are examined, successes and failures evaluated, and prospects for the future explored.

Origins of Swedish Population Policy

Sweden has frequently been recognized as exemplifying a distinct societal model. Marques Childs's seminal work of the 1930s, *Sweden: The Third Way*, argued that Sweden had achieved a happy alternative between communism and capitalism.[2] In *Sweden, Prototype of Modern Society*, sociologist Richard Tomasson stated that "Sweden has come to approximate the ideal type of the modern industrial society to a greater extent than any other nation in the world."[3]

This distinct model has been shaped by Swedish Social Democracy. Unlike most other socialist and social democratic parties in Europe, the Swedish Social Democrats successfully resolved the economic and social problems of the Great Depression, marginalized extremism, and then built their own model of a welfare state.

The greatest test of Swedish Social Democracy was finding an answer to the Great Depression. Other socialist parties rarely succeeded. Some socialist parties were reluctant to participate in coalitions with the "bourgeois parties," either for tactical reasons or because of a lingering commitment to "revolutionary" change. A second and more important reason for failure was the widespread and deeply held belief that under capitalism the rules of the capitalist economy (i.e., classical liberal economics) had to be applied. Keynesian economics had not yet been developed. So socialists in government tried to balance the budget and maintain the stability of the currency, which was tied to the gold standard. These policies exacerbated the crisis. Yet, as parties representing the working class, which suffered from massive unemployment, they wanted to protect their constituents through continued financing of unemployment insurance. Theory and practice were at odds. That double bind forced the German Social Democratic Party out of the government in 1931, crippling the Weimar Republic. In Britain, the Labour Party split over financial and economic policy. The socialist-led French Popular Front's economic and financial policies also failed. In Belgium, the socialists developed a proactive strategy, based on economic planning, but some top leaders, like Hendrik de Man, who became a collaborator in 1940, were infected by the very extremism they fought.

It took great political courage and a deep understanding of economic issues to follow another course. In only a handful of Scandinavian nations did socialists develop and successfully implement alternative policies. The most notable example was Sweden, whose Social Democratic Workers' Party had "developed a long line of brilliant and creative leaders."[4] Together with their Agrarian Party partners, the Social Democratic government of 1932 was the first to initiate massive public works based on deficit spending that led to a sharp decline of unemployment and pulled Sweden out of depression. The pragmatic Swedes were closer to the supporters of the New Deal than to their European socialist brethren. Among the major contributors to the theoretical foundation of the Social Democrats' economic policies was Gunnar Myrdal.[5]

The Social Democrats became a hegemonic party in Sweden. They transformed Sweden and co-opted the bourgeois parties in the process so that even when they were out of government, their political rivals did not fundamentally alter their policies. Early on the Social Democrats abandoned the idea of socializing the means of production and, in the words of the noted sociologist Walter Korpi, established a historic compromise with capital:

> It was based on a formula of cooperation between the labour movement and the representatives of capital to increase economic growth. Decision-making in the sphere of production was largely left to capital. The labour movement undertook responsibilities for affecting distribution of the increasing product by political means … according to the criteria of social justice.[6]

The originality demonstrated in the Social Democrats' economic policies was paralleled by their demographic policies, which were far more radical than those of contemporaries. One reason is that Gunnar Myrdal, who provided much of the intellectual basis for the socialist government's radical economic policies, also designed (together with his wife, Alva Myrdal) the framework for a new pronatalist population policy in Sweden.

The Swedish total-fertility-rate (TFR) birth rate had been generally declining from around 4 at the beginning of the century to below 2.0 in the 1930s, hitting a low of 1.7 in 1935.[7] Before Myrdal, pronatalism was largely the province of conservatives, who opposed contraception and attributed lower birth rates to the contamination of modern social ideas and the erosion of women's traditional homemaker role. Reformers and leftists supported neo-Malthusianism; they believed that limiting population would advance social equality. The Myrdals were the first to create a new synthesis that was not only consistent but synergistic with the Social Democrats' economic and social policies. In the words of Allan Carlson, a student, but by no means an admirer, of the Myrdals: "The Myrdals successfully wrestled the population issue away from Swedish conservatives and nationalists and turned it towards the service of socialist goals. In a remarkable 4-year period, they implemented a large share of their ideological program and helped transform the nature of the Swedish domestic state."[8] Carlson adds that "their socialist pronatalist program grew out of their independent work, without significant influence from other European sources."[9] This was a uniquely Swedish experiment; the Myrdals were its intellectual architects as well as key political players in its development.

In her book *Nation and Family*, Alva Myrdal wrote that dealing with the population question required "nothing less than a complete social redirection.... A population program must work itself into the whole fabric of social life and must interpenetrate and be interpenetrated by all other measures of social change."[10] Gunnar and Alva Myrdal's 1934 book *Kris i befolkningsfragan* (*Crisis in the Population Question*) launched the debate over the Swedish population question and made it a national issue. The book became a best seller. Its nine major arguments are summarized, as follows, in

Population: A Problem for Democracy, based on lectures Gunnar Myrdal delivered at Harvard in 1938 but somewhat revised in 1939 for publication.[11]

First, contraception has changed the relevance of Malthus. Malthus's ideas that population growth would outrun resources seemed to have rendered all social reform futile. Manchester liberalism, which incorporated Malthus's ideas, was inherently conservative and pessimistic. Social reform only became possible as a result of the development of contraception. Neo-Malthusianism was thus implicit in all liberal reformism; that is, social progress required keeping population down. The situation is now reversed; national interest and economic prosperity depend on increasing birth rates. The goal—even if not fully attainable—is a stable population.

Second, the need for a pronatalist policy makes possible a synthesis of leftist and conservative ideals. With declining birth rates, a population policy to increase birth rates becomes what one unnamed critic described as "the crowbar for social reform." The problem was how to get people to abstain from *not* reproducing. But this new situation also provided a basis for reconciling conservatives' commitment to the family and radicals' desire for social reform. The survival of the nation required conservatives to accept radical change "but also brings an explicit acceptance of some values dear to the conservative mind" by reformers.

Third, contraception is a precondition for a modern pronatalist policy. In a democratic society, an increase in birth rates can only take place if it corresponds to the interest of individuals and not out of "duty" to the nation. Parenthood should be voluntary and children must be brought up under good conditions.

Fourth, success of any pronatalist policy requires acceptance that ways must be found "to allow married women both to work and have a career and at the same time to have children."[12]

Fifth, children are an economic burden for their family. The interests of the individual and society are in contradiction. "The problem is that today children constitute an increased economic burden rather than a source of income or a means of support in old age."

Thus, argued Myrdal, the precondition to higher birth rates was that "a large part of the economic burden of bringing up children must be passed from the individual family to society as a whole."[13] Redistribution of wealth must take place not only between rich and poor but also between those with few or no children and those with many (horizontal redistribution).

Sixth, a successful population policy involves eliminating the obstacles that prevent ordinary people from following their wishes to marry and have children. This is exactly what demographers now stress: the need to create conditions to narrow the gap between desired number of children and actual number of children.

Seventh, the quality of population is just as important or even more important than the quantity. This involves providing children with better housing, nutrition, health care, and education. Thus "equalizing of the economic level" goes hand in hand with increased birth rates. Pronatalist aims therefore come together with social policy. Development of social policy "arises quite independently of the population crisis, but the population crisis comes at a very timely stage and constitutes a strong stimulus for reforms of a sort which have social and economic purposes within themselves."[14] In short, efforts at population policy are at one with the creation of a welfare state. The Myrdals also supported improving the quality of population through sterilization of those unfit to be parents, not for racial reasons, but because of mental retardation. (The Social Democrats believed that sterilization was consistent with their views on social engineering. The sterilization law was not abrogated until 1975.)[15]

Eighth, programs must be universal rather than means tested, providing services rather than cash grants. This became a fundamental principle of Swedish policy on support for families.

Ninth, reforms would take place over an extended time frame and go far beyond the relatively limited reforms achieved in the 1930s. "General opinion is certainly not ready for more far-reaching reforms. . . . There is . . . reason to expect that for some time there will be a certain diminution in interest in the population problem. The problem, however, will again come to the fore, and then in a more definite way. In this later period distribution reform of quite another magnitude will probably become possible. But even these reforms, which in fact would comprise a radical alteration in the whole social structure, probably cannot completely eliminate the differential cost of having children."[16] Functions from the "quasi-paternalistic family" must be transferred to the "wider national household."[17] Myrdal was right that many of Sweden's family policy reforms did not occur until the 1960s and 1970s. By 1938, the threat of war resulted in the need for increased defense spending and the temporary end of the reforms.

As a result of *Kris*, population policy became an important issue in Sweden and a central issue for the Social Democrats. In 1935, Prime Minister Per Albin Hansson stated that it was the most serious issue facing Sweden.[18] He appointed a Royal Population Commission of which Gunnar Myrdal was the leading member. The commission produced an impressive series of detailed reports that were followed up by legislation in 1937–38. This legislation included financial support for housing large families, prenatal care and subsidized delivery, a maternity bonus, and marriage loans. It lifted the ban on contraception and prohibited dismissing women from employment for reasons of marriage, pregnancy, or childbearing.[19] In addition, women were given the right to a twelve-week maternity leave. The commission reports were very much in the spirit of Myrdal's thinking. Of course, a shortage of money limited what could be done quickly.

There was a creative tension between the ideas of Gunnar Myrdal and Alva Myrdal. Gunnar Myrdal's preoccupation was maintaining the Swedish birth rate. This justified radical changes in Swedish society that in any case Gunnar, as a socialist, favored. Alva's major interest was not population policy but feminism. Her goal was the creation of full equality for women and the transformation of the family structure with greater emphasis on collective child rearing.[20] In the course of time, the stated goal of population policy in Sweden was largely superseded by the quest for full gender equality. Policies favoring gender equality helped sustain a relatively high birth rate. The rhetorical emphasis shifted from population policy to gender equality, but the two goals were really one, as Sommestad's previous comments demonstrate.

After World War II, Sweden, like most of the West, experienced a population boom. There was a brief resurgence of the male bread-winner model. But by the 1970s, the boom was over and birth rates declined precipitously. Women were needed in the workforce. Together with their coalition partners, the Social Democrats returned to the ideas of the Myrdals and implemented a program to increase birth rates and promote gender equality that constitutes the basis of today's policies.

Swedish Population Policy Today

The Swedish birth rate is close to—but not fully at—replacement level. For women born in the twentieth century the cohort fertility has remained about two children. Most women have two children, some have more, and relatively few—by comparative standards—have none. Nonetheless, without immigration, by 2030 deaths would exceed births.[21]

What is unusual about Sweden is the contrast between the stability of cohort fertility and the "rollercoaster fluctuations" of yearly birth rates measured by the TFR.[22] These fluctuations are not due to forces of nature but, ironically, constitute testimony to the fact that public policy does indeed affect women's behavior: "The great undulations in Swedish fertility are largely self-induced by the tight links between parenthood benefits and preceding income from a woman's own labor-force participation."[23] Changes in policies and benefits have been followed by changes in behavior.

What is indeed remarkable is that cohort fertility has remained stable despite significant changes in the age of childbearing and in the nature of the family structure. The mean age of childbearing has continually increased—it is now about thirty. Women are having the same number of children but having them later. This is significant because it challenges the common idea that one reason for the decline in birth rates is that women have children later. That is not the case in Sweden. At the same time, divorce has increased, marriage has declined, and cohabitation has become normal.

SUPPORT FOR PARENTS AND CHILDREN

Nations seeking to promote pronatalism have, in the words of Peter McDonald, a choice of "tools" from their "toolbox."[24] The choice of tools corresponds to the nation's political, social, economic, and cultural orientation. Sweden has a basically single-track system that is clear and simple. Sweden does not provide cash payments, tax benefits, lump-sum payments, or loans. This kind of support is more typical of societies that emphasize market capitalism approaches. Instead, Sweden's approach is consistent with its welfare state orientation.

It would seem that the reason for Sweden's relatively high birth rate is that Swedish women continue to desire an average of more than two children and the Swedish welfare state has removed much of the stress, financial and otherwise, that normally accompanies child rearing and might discourage potential parents. The goal is to decrease the gap between desired and actual fertility.

But the Swedish system does more than encourage and support fertility. It also determines the way in which fertility expresses itself. It constitutes a form of social engineering that shapes how childbearing occurs, the role of parents, gender relations, and the nature of the family. At the heart of the Swedish approach is a commitment to gender equality. The system is based on an earner-carer model in which both parents normally work and in which the father takes an active part in parenting.[25] In 2006, 76.3 percent of Swedish women of working age actually were employed, making Sweden the European Union country with the highest female labor participation except for Denmark. Many mothers in Sweden work only part time, however.

Sweden provides generous parental leave for working parents, whether married or not. Parental benefit in Sweden consists of 480 days—240 for the mother and 240 for the father. Days can be transferred between parents, but 60 days each cannot be transferred. A parent with joint custody of a child has a right to half of the days of parental benefit. Parental benefit consists of two different kinds of days, 390 of which are income related and 90 of which are given out at a flat rate of SEK 180 a day ($26).[26] Parental leave offers 80 percent of income up to SEK 424,000 ($62,096). Those with higher incomes may benefit from supplementary insurance plans. But the system was not especially generous to those who do not work: until recently, "parents with low income or no income at all receive parental benefits at a basic level of SEK 180 per day."

Parental leave encourages fathers to share in parenting through nontransferable paid leave of two months (the "daddy month")—an offer that is hard to refuse and clearly is meant to implicate fathers in a child-caring role early on. It is often concentrated in the summer, however, "an outcome that undercuts the ideological component in the policy to enhance men's role as caretakers of children." Division of parental leave also reflects the fact that the higher earner of a couple usually takes less leave.[27] Fathers also receive ten days of benefits annually for each child (so-called "daddy days"). There are also housing allowances for parents with children living at home, but they apply only to people with very low incomes. A second major benefit provided by the state is substantial family sick leave, up to 120 days a year, which is available to mothers or fathers.

A 2009 study by the Center for Economic and Policy Research in Washington shows that among twenty-one advanced nations, Sweden provides the longest paid leave for parents (tied with Germany) and also the greatest amount of nontransferable paid leave specifically targeting fathers. Sweden was first on their gender equality index.[28] Some have argued that Scandinavian gender equality is really "gender equality lite" insofar as women take far more parental leave than husbands and are more likely to work part time after giving birth. The Swedish system thus pretty much guarantees that children will be cared for by their own parents during the first year, and that the father will play an important role in child rearing from the outset. Most children then go on to preschool, open to children who are one year old.

The preschool system is another important reason why Swedish parents feel secure about having children. The Swedish preschool model is universalist. There is no shortage of facilities—they are intended for everyone—and they are of high quality and easily accessible. Hours are long and flexible. The personnel are skilled; each facility has teachers with tertiary degrees in early childhood education. There is a national curriculum for the schools. The Swedes insist that theirs is not child care, but preschool, and that it offers an indispensable educational base for development and promotes social equality and social integration. The ideal is to socialize children of all income levels and backgrounds. Unlike many American parents, who feel guilty if they do not stay home with their children, Swedish parents would more likely feel irresponsible if they failed to send their children to preschool. The largest part of the cost of preschool is borne by the state; the parents pay a small percentage, around 20 percent. Most preschools are run by municipalities, but there are also subsidized schools run as cooperatives. High schools and universities are free. In short, Swedish policy has incorporated the Myrdals' argument that the national community must become the extended family and that the nation must assume the cost of raising and educating children.

Parental leave policy is one of the factors that results in the increasing age of childbearing and the volatility of the TFR. Because parental leave is a percentage of salary, it is in the financial interest of young people to establish themselves, complete education, and advance in the workplace *before* having children. Because the right of parents to return to their job is guaranteed, as well as the right to part-time work, prospective parents may be encouraged to attain the job they want before having children. If an economic crisis occurs, parenting may be delayed, resulting in a decline in the TFR that is usually recuperated later on.

A parental leave system strictly tied to income could have delayed the timing of second or subsequent children. It was likely that after a first child, a woman might work part time and would delay a second pregnancy until she returned to full-time work. The result might be a very late pregnancy or no second child at all. The government therefore initiated a "speed premium" in 1980. A woman having another child within thirty months of the first is automatically eligible to receive the same maternity leave payment as the previous time and so on for subsequent births. Women have adapted their childbirth tempo to the policy.

As Paul Demeny argues, the earner-carer model is self-reinforcing:

> The declared aim of the most closely fertility-relevant social policies in Sweden, and in varying degrees also elsewhere in Western Europe, is to make participation of women in the formal labor force compatible with raising children. Few social policies enjoy greater unqualified support from demographers and sociologists than those seeking to achieve that objective. Indeed, fertility differences between Western European countries are routinely explained by differential success of government policies supporting compatibility. Economists also tend to concur in supporting the policy, if for somewhat different, macro-economic reasons: greater mobilization of the female labor force provides a degree of correction for the increasingly disadvantageous ratio between those in the labor force and those retired. On the micro-level there are also good reasons for the policy. Once the proportion of families with two wage earners—such as husband and wife—becomes fairly large in an economy, the relative economic status of families with only one earner becomes more and more disadvantageous or even untenable, especially when dependent children are also present. Gradual collectivization of the costs of child raising (for example, through publicly financed family allocations and through provision of benefits in kind, such as free child care for preschool children through crèches [i.e., day care centers], kindergartens, and the like) represents a major approach to easing the conflict between working outside the home and having children. Financing such

services, however, requires imposition of heavier tax burdens, which, in turn, put further pressure on families to seek participation of more than one adult member of the household in the formal labor force. Thus the system is self reinforcing and the option that one of the parents stays at home with children until the children are grown (in practical terms for 20 to 25 years) can be plausibly exercised only by the exceptionally well-to-do, or those willing to deny to themselves and to their children material comforts that are customary in their social reference group.[29]

In the last few decades, however, the tide of an expanding welfare state has ebbed. From its inception, the Swedish welfare state recognized the importance of providing affordable housing to the population. (As we have seen, Gunnar Myrdal recognized the importance of adequate housing as a factor in population policy.) The financial crisis of the 1990s led Sweden, however, like many other European welfare states, to drastically cut housing subsidies to reduce public expenditures. Housing subsidies, therefore, no longer are part of the "toolbox" of public policy except on a limited basis for those with very low incomes. The consequences may be less access to affordable housing for those with lower or middle incomes and greater housing segregation.[30] It does not take much imagination to realize that this could have an impact not only on birth rates but also on the quality of children's development. Residential segregation by income and ethnicity could imperil the process of social integration as well.

Swedish family policies reflected the values of the dominant Social Democratic Workers' Party, values that were ultimately shared by some of the nonsocialist parties as well. The Social Democrats have ceased being hegemonic since the 1990s. Since 2006, Sweden has been governed by a nonsocialist coalition whose parties have divergent views on family policy. The Liberal Party follows the earner-carer consensus; the Christian Democrats represent a constituency of Pentecostal churches (the vast majority of Swedes are nonpracticing

Lutherans) and favor more traditional views supporting stay-at-home mothers. The coalition enacted two bills appealing to contradictory philosophies with the result that the laws themselves seem inconsistent.

The first bill reflects Liberal views. It established a gender equality bonus of SEK 13,500 ($1,977) for couples who share parental leave relatively equally. The second law, the Municipal Child Raising Allowance, constitutes a wedge driven into the last seventy years of family policy. It provides support for stay-at-home parents (presumably mostly mothers) for children between one and three years. They could receive up to 3,000 SEK ($439) a month per child not attending preschool. The support is channeled through municipalities who are "free to choose whether to introduce the allowances."[31] By autumn 2010 about 100 out of 290 municipalities had done so. Some scholars assert that this legislation poses a particular risk to the integration of "immigrant children with lowly educated parents."[32] It will be interesting to note whether the nonsocialist coalition, which was reelected in 2010, will further open up the breach within the existing family policy model. Given their lack of a clear majority, that may be unlikely.

THE FAMILY

The "traditional family" has ceased to exist as a recognized and favored intermediary institution between the state and individual. Swedish population and gender policies have played an important role in redefining the family, first by insisting on gender equality and creating conditions that encourage both men and women to work, and second by assuming strict neutrality concerning the form of family relations. Men and women, even if married, are taxed separately. Under such a system, "only the most economically irrational men would seek to keep their wives out of the labour market."[33] Lena Sommestad argues that the male breadwinner model was always weak in Sweden. Because of large-scale male emigration, women were an important part of the labor force. Marriage rates were very low (among women born in 1885–89 more than 50 percent never married).[34] And unlike in many other countries, men and women were protected by the same labor legislation.[35] In 1938, single mothers were afforded the same maternity benefits as married women. In 1971, income tax was no longer assessed jointly for a married couple but on a purely individual basis. Widow's pensions were phased out in 1989. The Cohabitation Act of 1987 established legal conditions concerning the joint property of cohabitants. Parents, whether married or unmarried, have responsibility for their children, and generally when their relationship dissolves, maintain joint custody. The role—and responsibility—of the biological father has always been fundamental in Swedish law.[36]

It is difficult to measure the significance of the state's neutrality toward the form of relationships. One reason, perhaps, is that Statistics Sweden does not differentiate between married and cohabiting couples. Most children are born to a couple, whether married or cohabitating. Many cohabiting couples who have children subsequently marry after the first or second birth. The proportion of extramarital births in Sweden has been among the highest in Europe for decades, yet the share of births to single mothers has remained at around 10 percent except for in the mid-1990s. "Today, nearly 60 percent of all children and two-thirds of all first children are born in non-marital cohabiting relationships in Sweden."[37]

Childbirth tends to occur in the late twenties or early thirties; teenage pregnancy is very rare. Cohabitants may well be less committed to or certain about relationships than married couples. Some studies indicate that their economic situation is less secure: cohabitation is less enduring than marriage. But perhaps it is a matter of degree. If the trend in many countries is toward serial monogamy, that monogamy in Sweden may take the form of either marriage or cohabitation. The problem of reconstituted families among cohabiting couples in Sweden may not be fundamentally different from reconstituted families among divorced and remarried partners elsewhere. It remains to be seen whether cohabitation is an alternative to marriage, or, as Peter McDonald argues, a "pathway that promotes the institution of marriage in a riskier social environment.[38]

In Sweden, cohabitation with children, like marriage, is governed by public law. Rather than an alternative to marriage, perhaps it would be better qualified as "marriage lite."

Thus, whereas at first glance Swedish neutrality toward the form of the family may appear highly significant, it is not clear whether it is so significant in practice. As noted previously, former Social Democratic minister of the environment Lena Sommestad wrote: "It has furthermore been shown that countries that do not stigmatize non-marital cohabitation or extra-marital births have a better chance of maintaining higher fertility rates. Since there is a decline in the marriage rate all over the industrialized world with later and fewer marriages and more divorces, non-marital births are needed to compensate." It is not clear whether Swedish policy is merely a recognition of this social reality or a means of justifying or even encouraging it. One important difference between Sweden and the United States is that in Sweden, unlike the United States, there are few single mothers and very few teenage pregnancies. In Sweden, out-of-wedlock births are generally conscious choices of women in their late twenties or thirties.

FINANCES

Sweden spends a lot of money on children. Studies indicate that Sweden spends 22.9 percent of per capita gross domestic product (GDP) on children under 15, the highest percentage among countries that belong to the Organization for Economic Cooperation and Development. Spending on children's education from birth to twenty years constitutes 31.2 percent of per capita GDP, exceeded only by Denmark. Finally, Sweden balances its spending between children and the elderly in a child-friendly way. The elderly-child ratio (ratio of spending on old people versus children) is 1.2.[39]

In financial terms, keeping the Swedish model viable requires adequate economic growth, continued solvency of the pension system, an acceptable dependency ratio between the working and nonworking population, a relatively high birth rate, and immigration that can compensate for less than replacement-level birth rates. Because of the financial crisis of the 1990s, the Swedish government rethought the scope and nature of its programs. The pension system was reformed from a defined benefit system to a notional system based on paying as you go and a privately managed financial account scheme. Housing subsidies were drastically cut. The core roles of the welfare state were redefined and limited in order to allow for its survival.

The Swedish government considers that under current conditions, an acceptable dependency ratio can be maintained far into the future. Increasing longevity will slowly raise the number of older people, but this trend can be compensated for by a slow and incremental increase of the retirement age. This in turn rests on another assumption: that in the Swedish political system, decisions like raising the retirement age are not politicized and public opinion will continue to support generous policies executed by technocratic means and will not be tempted by the siren songs of neoliberalism that have resonated throughout much of the world. Of course, external economic and financial crises can impact and undermine the Swedish equilibrium, requiring adjustments that would be unfavorable.

Sweden can afford its generous and costly parental policies because it is a highly competitive economy. Sweden comes in second on the World Economic Forum's Global Competitiveness Report for 2010–2011, just behind Switzerland and ahead of Singapore and the United States. It is among the top five nations in such areas as institutions, higher education and training, goods marketing efficiency, technological readiness, business sophistication, and innovation. Sweden more than compensates for the "most problematic factors for doing business," which, not surprisingly, are restrictive labor regulations, tax rates, and tax regulations.[40]

IMMIGRATION

Some countries that are threatened by lowest-low birth rates, like Singapore, pursue a self-conscious policy of seeking immigrants in order to increase the workforce and achieve the goals of their population policy. Sweden needs immigration to maintain a stable population in the long term, but immigration policy today is not defined around such a perceived need. Until 1975, Sweden fostered immigration based on the requirements of its labor market. And since EU expansion in 2004, there has been renewed labor force immigration due to free movement of labor within the EU. But today most immigration to Sweden consists of those seeking asylum (as well as family reunification). The explicit rationale for accepting these immigrants is humanitarian. It is not clear to what extent there may also be an unstated desire to bring in low-paid workers or increase the size of the workforce. The trade unions successfully stopped labor force immigration, but admission of asylum seekers circumvents that opposition by appealing to broad-based humanitarian values. Nonetheless, the result is striking: the proportion of those residents born in another country in 2008 was 13.8 percent, one of the highest figures in the EU. Because of their cultural background, lower levels of education, and reluctance for women to work, and also because of discrimination, many asylum seekers suffer from greater unemployment and require a disproportionate amount of welfare benefits. They are not easily integrated into the labor market and often end up in lower-paying jobs or in small-scale enterprises. Despite efforts to disperse asylum seekers throughout the country, many are concentrated in suburbs of large cities. Many are Moslem. The entry into Parliament of the xenophobic far-right Swedish Democrats in 2010 indicates that immigration has become an important political problem.

What is the impact of immigration on population? Clearly, immigration increases the population, but period trends "over time have been quite similar for Swedish- and foreign-born women."[41] But if that is the case, immigration will not produce significantly higher birth rates. Thus, in order to maintain a stable work force, immigration would have to continue. This, in turn, means further changes in the composition of Swedish society and may incite ongoing social and political tensions.

Sweden as a Model?

In his many excellent articles on the decline in fertility and policies to remedy it, Peter McDonald stresses that low levels of fertility in advanced countries today can be explained by incoherence arising from differences in levels of gender equality among social institutions:

> Very low fertility is the product of the combination of high gender equity in individual-oriented institutions with the persistence of only moderate gender equity in family-oriented institutions. . . . If women are provided with opportunities near to equivalent to those of men in education and market employment, but these opportunities are severely curtailed by having children, then, on average, women will restrict the number of children that they have to an extent which leaves fertility at a very low, long-term level.[42]

He also argues that market deregulation in neocapitalism has increased risks for workers, which undermines their willingness to engage in family formation. Young people must therefore be assured that "if they marry and have children they will be supported by the society. . . . Effectively this implies large public transfers from those who do not have the care of young children to those who do."[43]

This was precisely the insight in the 1930s of Gunnar Myrdal and Alva Myrdal, who fashioned foundations of Swedish population policy at a time when Sweden was reeling from the Great Depression. Swedish policy involves a redistribution of resources from those without children to those with and is based on the notion that society as a whole must take responsibility for raising children.

How successful then are Swedish population policies? Compared to the rest of Europe, they are very successful. Sweden's birth rate is one of the highest in Europe. Sweden is not facing a demographic crisis. Yet, despite outstanding programs of support to children, Sweden does not achieve replacement-level fertility. What more could Sweden possibly do?

The problem is, as Paul Demeny suggests, that raising actual birth rates to what women say they desire is not possible:

But do not fertility surveys confirm a preference expressed by a large majority of women, men, and families for having at least two children? Would it not follow, then, that regardless of whether a family policy is meant to be pronatalist or simply family- and people-friendly, its task is plain: to provide moral and material support so that families (or just women) can have the children that they wish to have? The answer to this question is also simple: expressed preferences concerning the number of children desired may well be genuine, but they are also in competition with other preferences the satisfaction of which is, at least in principle, attainable in modern societies. The outcome of such competition is not necessarily in favor of children. The children actually born may turn out to be what in the title of one of his novels Günter Grass called *Kopfgeburten*, births that occur in the minds of their would-be parents.[44]

Yet even with replacement-level fertility, Sweden would face an aging population and a growing dependency ratio. This could only be mitigated by a rising birth rate, but the idea of a long-term TFR above 2.1 is almost unimaginable.

The vulnerabilities to this system are the continued success of the Swedish economy, financial stability, and the willingness of governments and the population to pay high taxes. Will Swedes continue to support their welfare state against the temptations of neoliberal solutions? This is important because, as McDonald points out, the market in general penalizes rather than rewards having children. Do the modest changes introduced by the conservative government in the direction of freedom of choice mark the beginning of the end of the Swedish system or do they constitute a bump in the road, in the sense that the earner-carer model is so strongly established that behavior will not be changed? Another vulnerability is rising opposition to Sweden's immigration policies, because Sweden is dependent on immigration to maintain a stable population, but its immigration policies are not work related.

Groups from low–birth rate countries frequently visit Sweden to study the Swedish approach to pronatalism. To what extent is the Swedish model applicable to other nations? The Swedish model is certainly similar to that of other Nordic societies. All of them have similar policies and relatively high birth rates. All are wealthy, advanced postindustrial nations and share a common history, similar social structure and values, and Protestant heritage. They all are committed to social equality and social solidarity. They are characterized by weak families as defined by Reher; that is, the individual and individual values tend to have priority over the family group.[45] With the exception of Finland, their languages are mutually comprehensible and they have influenced each other from the beginning of their history. Until recent immigration, they were quite homogenous societies, not greatly divided by religion, language, or ethnicity.

It is not likely that Swedish policy will be a good model for most countries with low birth rates. It is based on the acceptance of modern, secularist values, including gender equality and nontraditional family structures. It presupposes faith in a decisionmaking process based on a technocratic, social engineering approach to policy. The first characteristic limits the applicability of the Swedish model because many societies are far from accepting family policy dissociated from marriage. Certainly Italy, Japan, and Singapore have value systems that are incompatible with Sweden's. Nor do many nations live up to the second characteristic, the reputation for state incorruptibility and competence, which justifies public faith in Sweden's approach to social engineering.

CHAPTER TWO

Demography in France: From National Security to Family-Work Reconciliation

In losing the demographic hegemony of Europe, France inexorably regressed from the status of great power to that of a middle power. Despite the severity of the two first shocks against Germany [Franco-Prussian War and World War I], French opinion had for a long time cradled itself in an illusion concerning the comparative power of its country. It nourished itself on clichés of past glory; maintained in the cult of a bypassed grandeur, it rested on the conviction of a pretended moral superiority, when it didn't abandon itself to the sweet comfort that could be procured from the Maginot line. Between the state of mind and the facts, the gap was enormous.

—JEAN-CLAUDE CHESNAIS, "LA POLITIQUE DE LA POPULATION FRANÇAISE DEPUIS 1914"[1]

MODERN FRANCE HAS BEEN SHAPED by its response to defeat. France suffered two existential defeats in seventy years, the Franco-Prussian War of 1870–71 and the Battle of France of 1940. The former raised the question of whether France would remain a great power, and the latter whether it would even survive as a sovereign state in control of its traditional frontiers.

Each of these defeats was perceived as having roots in demography. France was the first country to undergo the demographic transition; it went from being the most populous nation in Western Europe in the eighteenth century to having fewer people than Germany, Britain, or Austria-Hungary in 1914.

French concerns about demography arose specifically in terms of national security. French defeat in the Franco-Prussian War of 1870–71 transformed France's low birth rate into a political issue because France's archenemy, Germany, was experiencing rapid population growth. The combined German population was about the same as that of France in 1870; by 1914 it was half again as large. This put France at a disadvantage in mobilizing an army as large as Germany's. Demography could easily become a monocausal explanation for French defeat, as shown in the above Chesnais quotation. Yet despite the urgings of "depopulationists," the Third Republic did not take meaningful steps toward a pronatalist policy until the very eve of World War II. Surprisingly, just before hostilities began, the otherwise hapless Daladier government enacted a decree law that constituted the basis for a new family policy. To be sure, the law was larded with the kind of punitive measures against contraception and abortion that pronatalists had long been demanding (and was repealed several decades later). But there was something new in the law—financial support for large families. The collaborationist Vichy regime continued family allowances and supported the family as a pillar of the authoritarian state.

At the Liberation from the Nazis, France's stagnant or even declining birth rate was now seen as causally related to the lack of dynamism of the French economy and French society as a whole. France, it seemed, was the victim of Malthusianism. How to escape from the grips of a stalemate society? That question was on the minds of Resistance and postwar political leaders. The solution was the creation of a new paradigm—a *dirigiste* welfare state, with significant pronatalist dimensions. The *trente glorieuses* followed (thirty years of economic growth after World War II), which modernized the French economy, along with the baby boom.

In recent years, French birth rates have achieved near-replacement levels. France would seem to be a model for advanced societies suffering from low birth rates. The total French population before World War II stagnated at about 40 million; today it is about 63 million. According to recent projections by the Institut nationale de la statistique et des études économiques, it should reach about 74 million in 2060.[2]

Population policy was shaped in the atmosphere of the Liberation. The international situation has changed since then; no longer an existential enemy, Germany became France's key partner in the European Union. Pronatalism still undergirds French policy, but that policy now focuses on supporting gender equality, reconciling the role of women as workers and mothers, and protecting French children and families against poverty.

From *Grande Nation* to Insecure Power: The Price of the Demographic Transition

France's power in the preindustrial age was a result of its abundant natural resources, centralized government, and large population. During the reign of Louis XIV, France sought, and on several occasions nearly achieved, hegemony in Europe. Benefiting from the rise of nationalism and the invention of the mass citizen army, Napoleon almost achieved the dominance that had eluded the kings.

French national power declined in the nineteenth century because of political instability and frequent regime change. Unlike Britain, France did not undergo early and rapid industrialization. The French population was stable while that of the rest of Europe rapidly expanded. There was, however, little consciousness of decline. France remained a nation of small holdings owned by peasant proprietors who had every interest in restricting the number of offspring to avoid division of the land. Lack of significant industrialization limited the pull of the cities for the rural lower class. There was little improvement of agricultural productivity in the first half of the century.

Unlike Britain, social mobility for the urban population was not based on a new, rapidly expanding industrial economy created by the entrepreneurial spirit, but rather on social climbing. The ambitious young men of Balzac's novels who flocked to Paris from the provinces sought riches and power, but Rastignac was certainly not looking for a managerial position in a textile mill. Industrialization did accelerate during the French Second Empire, but there was no take-off similar to Britain's. Social mobility required investment of a family's limited resources in a single son.

It was almost as if there were two economic and demographic models in the early nineteenth century, exemplified by Britain and France. In the former, industrialization was early and the demographic transition late; the inverse was true in the latter.[3] But France was the exception in Europe. The French peasants and lower middle class practiced neo-Malthusianism without having read Malthus. In the words of demographer Jean-Pierre Bardet, "The relative decline of French population had only one cause: the individual wish of the French, in a decision reconfirmed from one generation to another throughout the nineteenth century to limit the number of their descendants."[4] This was accomplished first by late marriage and then through contraception. Contraception first became popular in urban areas, but soon permeated the countryside as well. The dominant form of contraception seems to have been coitus interruptus. "The collapse of natality observed from 1790 to 1850 did not therefore constitute a true and modern demographic transition, but the pursuit, by other means, of the old agrarian Malthusianism."[5]

The practice of controlling population through contraception was condoned by the Church. Bardet cites the reply of a Roman tribunal in 1816 to a French cleric: "A woman can have relations even if she knows from experience that her husband will ejaculate outside the vagina, if in refusing she would be badly seen by her husband."[6]

Neo-Malthusianism was advocated by leading economists like Jean-Baptiste Say: "Men should be encouraged to produce savings rather than babies. . . . Savings permit families to consume, beyond the income of their industry, of their work, of their talents, still another income, that of their capital."[7] During the Second Empire, some thinkers stressed the relationship of lower birth rates and improved standards of living. The argument was that increased consumption led to a decline in birth rates. As the standard of living of workers rose they would have fewer children and rise up to the middle classes, thereby assuring social stability.[8] In short, French thinking in the mid–nineteenth century tended to see the decline of birth rates through contraception as desirable. There was congruence between the individual's pursuit of his perceived self-interest and the good of the nation. These values parallel much of today's thinking.

Not until 1866—Austria's defeat in the Austro-Prussian War—was there an intimation that relative population decline could have a deleterious effect on national power. Before 1866, Germany was hopelessly divided. Italy began unification in 1859–60, but it was weak. Because the Austrian Empire was a ramshackle affair, the French had little difficulty in defeating Austria in 1859. Russia was still backward, as shown by its defeat in the Crimean War. Despite occasional tensions, French governments avoided conflict with the most modern European state, Britain, which, in any case, was focused on imperial expansion and whose vital interest on the continent was maintaining a balance of power to prevent the emergence of a hegemon. Only after Prussia's victory at Sadowa in 1866 did the geopolitical situation change rapidly. Indeed, were it not for the fact that France was part of a highly competitive European state system, it could be argued that there was nothing inherently wrong in France's choice of a neo-Malthusian economic and demographic model. But France's defeat of 1870–71 in the Franco-Prussian War demonstrated that there was a conflict between the interests of the individual and the interests of the nation. How could it be reconciled?

From One Defeat to Another (1870–1940): The Rise of Pronatalism

This general ascension, this phenomenon of capillarity [social mobility], is only possible in a country with political equality and economic inequality, because everyone has the same rights to fortune; one only has to conquer it in a struggle of atrocious egotism.

—ÉMILE ZOLA[9]

The seventy years that followed defeat in the Franco-Prussian War saw the rise of a pronatalist movement with remarkably little effect on birth rates. This experience is relevant today in explaining why awareness of a population problem does not necessarily lead to an effective policy response. The explanation lies in strong social forces that make smaller families desirable—and the failure of pronatalists to devise an effective strategy that takes such concerns into account.

There is no mystery as to why birth rates remained low.[10] They were an integral part of what Stanley Hoffmann called France's "stalemate society," a society based on stability, not growth. Protectionism was a perfect reflection of the defensive nature of society. Having few children was a logical response to socioeconomic realities but was not compatible with the interests of the nation as a whole. The need for a population policy was obviated to some extent by immigration and the empire. Just like the United States (albeit on a smaller scale), France attracted and assimilated large numbers of foreigners. The republican creed made it possible to absorb immigrants who were willing to become French on an individual level by accepting French language, culture, and values. Some of the needs of industry were also filled by workers from the colonies. The colonies also provided large numbers of soldiers in World War I and World War II. One of the reasons for the expansion of the French empire after 1871 was to compensate for defeat and to create the belief that there were a hundred million Frenchmen (all of whom could be drafted even though less than half of them could vote).

In 1896, the Alliance nationale pour l'accroissement de la population française was founded. This organization was influential but not very successful at the time. It was republican, not clericalist, and distinct from familialist groups tied to the Church. For example, Arsène Dumont, whose book *Dépopulation et civilisation* was especially influential, suggested that one way to increase population was to end the celibacy of the clergy! The Alliance was concerned above all by the German threat. Before World War I, its approach was primarily moralist, but its argument could easily be interpreted by skeptics as calling for more children to serve as cannon fodder.

Let us first look briefly at the arguments made by pronatalists and examine why their passionate concerns were not translated into legislation. We can take as an example Paul Leroy-Beaulieu (not an Alliance leader), a noted liberal economist who taught at the École libre des sciences politiques and was named to a chair at the Collège de France. His brother was Anatole Leroy-Beaulieu, a Catholic liberal who had published on Russia, defended Dreyfus, and written one of the most important philo-Semitic works of the nineteenth century, *Israël chez les nations.*

Leroy-Beaulieu's somewhat long-winded book, *La question de la population* (1913), provides a good analysis of the causes of declining fertility that he attributed to two major causes: children were no longer profitable; and the "development of education, personal and familial ambition, democratic ideas, [and] harsher competition in diverse careers."[11]

For Leroy-Beaulieu, the goal was a norm of three children per family. His policy prescriptions, however, explain why pronatalist advocates did not get far in France. They include restoration of religious belief and an end to the government's antireligious campaigns; repression of "immoral propaganda," that is, advocacy of contraception; severe punishment of abortions (and removing trials from too-lenient juries); ending education for the lower classes by age thirteen or fourteen so that children could go to work sooner; government subsidies and benefits, such as housing subsidies, restricted to families with at least three children; plural votes for fathers of at least three children; public-sector jobs only for fathers of three or more children; and 1 year rather than 3 of military service for fathers of three or more children. Leroy-Beaulieu after all, had tipped his hand by referring to *arrivisme,* which is the way the socially established deprecated social mobility aspirations of the lower classes. Many of these recommendations would have been politically toxic under the Republic but found favor (briefly) under the Vichy regime.

The Third Republic was a democratic regime with universal male suffrage. There was little likelihood that voters with fewer than three children would countenance legislation that went against their interests and values. With the exception of bonuses for third children, the approach was purely punitive. Leroy-Beaulieu, as a (nineteenth-century) liberal economist, could not imagine a welfare state that would redistribute large amounts of money to provide benefits to parents—nor could the political class.[12] The only significant pieces of legislation enacted before World War I (1913) provided maternity aid and some limited financial aid to families with three or more children.[13]

But pronatalism was not restricted to the (republican) right. France's leading public intellectual and liberal iconoclast Émile Zola wrote his mammoth novel *La fécondité* between August 1898 and May 1899 in England (where he had taken refuge to escape arrest after publishing "J'Accuse," his famous open letter charging a cover-up in the Dreyfus Affair). *La fécondité* is a nineteenth-century version of a docudrama. As a novel, it is certainly lacking; the plot is episodic and the characters wooden. But what stands out is Zola's depiction of the determination of nineteenth-century French society to restrict conception in order to achieve social mobility (*capillarité*, the term he borrows from Arsène Dumont) and the ways that it was done. There is no comparable account of how sexual "fraud" was practiced, the underground world of abortion, how unwanted children were disposed of, the deleterious impact of wet nursing, and the use of hysterectomies to make sex possible without risk. In the novel, these practices lead to disaster—characters die from abortions, lose their vitality from hysterectomies, and unwanted children given away become murderers. All those whose lives are based on "defrauding" nature finish badly. On the other hand, the hero and heroine, Mathieu and Marianne Froment, who give themselves up to a life based on fertility, who return to the soil and refuse to practice contraception, create a huge, triumphant, unstoppable family. They become a force of nature (literally) that symbolizes a new and vital France, cultivating supposedly uncultivable lands and sending children on to the colonies.

Throughout history, there has not been a single step forward, without [the force of] numbers having pushed humanity on its march. Tomorrow, like today, will be conquered by the swarming of crowds in search of happiness. And those will be the benefits awaited by our age—economic equality finally obtained as was political equality, a fair division of wealth rendered henceforth easy, obligatory work reestablished in its glorious necessity.[14]

Whatever the limits of Zola's argument, he seems to have recognized the need to escape from the straitjacket of Malthusianism, that economic and demographic growth and social justice could act synergistically.

After World War I, there was greater realization that effective pronatalist policies required government funding. The war, which required raising vast sums of money and creating big government on a temporary basis, may have convinced elites that a larger state role could be justified in matters of national security. Pronatalists also recognized that although having children was a duty, society needed to provide a "just distribution of expenses."[15] The problem was that they advocated punitive policies against bachelors and small families as well as benefits restricted to large families, which offended the notion of "republican equality." They also strongly supported repressive policies against contraception and abortion and restrictions on divorce. The pronatalist camp suffered from oversimplification, hypocrisy, hysteria, and demographic determinism, traits that proved rather enduring.

Perhaps the most thoughtful advocate of pronatalism was Alphonse Landry, a senator who served several times as a minister in the interwar period. In his classic work of theory, *La Révolution démographique*, Landry attributed the decline of birth rates to "the rationalization of life."[16] He did not believe that this decline would necessarily end in a new equilibrium, however.[17] To remedy the decline of birth rates, he supported legislation, including what would later be called horizontal redistribution.[18]

The propaganda of the pronatalists was at loggerheads with the spirit of Third Republic France, which in many ways was very modern. At least for those with some degree of economic means (and even for those without), pleasure, especially sexual pleasure, was an inherent part of life. The state was not expected to interfere in private life nor to interfere with sexual freedom. Pronatalism did not monopolize public debate. Neo-Malthusianism also had its public advocates. But one suspects that the *esprit railleur* was even more effective; it was too easy to point out the contrast between the bombastic proclamations of the pronatalists and how few children they had! And once the Great Depression set in with mass unemployment, the argument that France needed more children—to produce more unemployed workers—would not have gone uncontested.

The French political system during the Third Republic was based on the concept of limited government. A political system that strove to keep taxes low was not likely to have the means to encourage people to have more children. Nor was a limited but democratic government able to compel people to have more children. (One is reminded of Jack Benny's story of being accosted by a robber who told him he had to choose between his money and his life. Like Benny, Third Republic leaders needed more time to think about it.)

By 1939, the pronatalist moment had arrived. As the international situation darkened, so did the political mood. A crescendo of public opinion developed that reflected a political consensus.[19] This was in part a change in the approach of the Alliance, which, in the course of the interwar period, had little by little minimized nationalist and militarist propaganda and focused more on social justice, specifically criticizing the de facto penalization of large families.[20]

The government was committed to act, doubtless inspired by the international context—Italy and Germany were already promoting pronatalism. When the Daladier government, influenced especially by minister of finance Paul Reynaud, decided to create the Haut comité de la population, its five members included top Alliance activists who were also influential parliamentarians or high civil servants. Georges Pernot and Alphonse Landry were senators and former ministers, Philippe Serre was a deputy, Frédéric Roujou was on the Conseil d'État, and Fernand Boverat was president of the

Alliance.[21] The committee was administratively attached to the Secretariat-General of the prime minister. It provided a report to Daladier that constituted the basis for his decree law of July 29 that became known as the Family Code.[22]

The code established the doctrinal content of France's first wave of state intervention; it created the institutional base and recruited the administrators who directed policy in the final months of the Third Republic. Many of them remained under Vichy and continued during de Gaulle's Provisional Government and the Fourth Republic. In the words of one scholar, "It was the crisis of 1939, followed by a catastrophic defeat, a four-year foreign occupation, and a hopeful liberation, that laid the foundations of modern French demographic policy," which involved "the beginning of a direct and *permanent* involvement of the state in these areas."[23]

The July 29, 1939, decree-law, titled Relative to the Family and French Natality, included provisions against pornography, alcoholism, contraceptive devices, and public advocacy of contraception.[24] To circumvent lenient juries, it eliminated jury trials for abortion. None of this was exactly groundbreaking (much of it recalls Leroy-Beaulieu), but it did reflect the moralistic tone of much of the pronatalist movement. The minister of the interior, Albert Sarraut, had to intervene to block efforts to make abortion a crime against national security![25]

This legislation established some of the basic principles of French population policy: support for natality and compensation for the burden on the family, that is, horizontal redistribution. It reflected a national consensus—even the Communist Party supported it. The Family Code created universal incentives to provide support for children. These included bonuses for the first child, which totaled about two months' worth of the average salary. Family allowances were made universal from the second child on. For every second child, the parents received at least 10 percent of the average salary in the geographic department on a regular basis, and 20 percent for the third child and all children thereafter. This was a significant amount of money. The legislation placed great stock in keeping families on the land, perhaps hoping that this would encourage population growth. It provided for loans to young farmers of 5,000 to 20,000 francs. Obviously influenced by the nineteenth-century conservative theorist Pierre-Frédéric Guillaume le Play's argument that equal division of a parent's land among children had lowered birth rates, it increased the share of agricultural land inherited by a son who worked the land. In addition, the law provided assistance to fathers who lacked the means to support their children, facilitated the adoption process, and mandated teaching demography in school. Financing would come from a tax surcharge on the childless. In addition, inheritance taxes would be reduced for people with three or more children.

The Family Code of 1939 was a long-term policy created as part of a war-preparedness effort. It was a response to the old argument that low birth rates had jeopardized French national defense. A month after the promulgation of the Family Code, France was at war. In May 1940, Germany invaded France; in a matter of weeks France was defeated. The Third Republic collapsed and an authoritarian regime was set up under Marshal Philippe Pétain in July 1940, the so-called Vichy regime (which received this name because it was established in Vichy, located in a part of France that was not occupied by the Germans in 1940). This regime pursued collaboration, believing that Germany's triumph was final. The Vichy government proclaimed a National Revolution aimed at undoing the legacy of the French Revolution and the Republic, restoring a France based on traditional values. Its slogan—"Work, Family, Fatherland" (Travail, Famille, Patrie)—contrasted markedly with Liberty, Equality, Fraternity. Although in many ways Vichy constituted the antithesis of the Third Republic, it continued the policies outlined in the Family Code.

Pétain's comment in a speech of June 20, 1940, that France's defeat was the result of "too few allies, too few weapons, too few babies" was a self-serving testimony to the strength of demographic determinism as an explanation for French defeat.[26] The credibility of the statement was based on decades of pronatalist propaganda.

Of course, it is true that low birth rates comprised one cause of France's weakness, but the defeat of 1940 was not the direct result of low birth rates. Had the French army not fought a war based on static defense, had it used its tanks and planes in a different way and made better use of modern communication, the Battle of France could have turned out differently. In short, if France's military had not followed the military strategy enforced by Pétain and his generation, France might not have fallen.

The Vichy regime continued to implement the Family Code and provide family allowances. But the motivations for this policy had changed. As we have seen, pronatalists before the war had wanted to strengthen France's military power. But the Vichy government accepted defeat as definitive. "The ideologues of the National Revolution presented *dénatalité* as a kind of retribution on industrial society, a blight brought on by secularization, urbanization and proletarianization. Their solution to the demographic problem formed a part of their larger vision of a return to a rural, preindustrial, Christian society."[27] The family would not function as a means of restoring French greatness, but as a part of a natural hierarchy on which the authoritarian État Française state was based. These advocates of the family came from a different political subculture than the pronatalists; the latter were basically secularist and conservative, whereas the former were Catholics who had never been happy with the Third Republic's secularist agenda.[28] For Vichy officials, the family headed by the paterfamilias represented the natural basis of a hierarchical, authoritarian society.

French Policy after the War

The Vichy regime's claim to represent France was contested by nationalist general Charles de Gaulle, who established Free France in London and worked together with the internal French Resistance. By 1944, the Vichy government was discredited. At the Liberation, de Gaulle's Provisional Government returned to France and assumed power.

De Gaulle was president of the Provisional Government until January 20, 1946, when he resigned because of his frustration with political parties. De Gaulle wanted a political system with strong executive authority; instead, a parliamentary system in many ways akin to the Third Republic was established. When this Fourth Republic collapsed in 1958, de Gaulle returned and created a Fifth Republic modeled on his own ideas.

Despite his short time in office after the war, de Gaulle was successful in laying the foundations for a different kind of France. De Gaulle's goal was to restore France's greatness. De Gaulle realized that this could only be done by radical transformation of the economy and society. In this respect, he shared many of the goals of the French Resistance, which also rejected the immobilism of Third Republic France. After World War II, the new France broke with the pessimism and brittleness of the Third Republic mindset in almost all areas, including culture.

Population policy would play its role together with economic planning, government intervention in the economy, and the creation of a social welfare state. Together, these efforts would lead to a new and energetic France. And such a France would be capable of pursuing an activist foreign policy and regaining its rank as a great power. French industry before the war had lagged behind Britain and Germany; protectionism rather than dynamism had been the order of the day. In the postwar era, banking, insurance, and several key industries were nationalized. A system of economic planning, known as the Monnet Plan after its author, would encourage long-term economic planning backed by government resources. Just as France would escape from economic stagnation, so too would it escape from population immobility. In short, population and family policy were congruent with social and economic policy in general. The state was to play a leading role in organizing production and redistributing wealth—and in promoting population growth. The relationship of all these would be synergistic. If, as Marie-Thérèse Letablier states, "the level of fertility in France is related to state support for families," the early days of Liberation, when the Provisional

Government under Charles de Gaulle defined population policy as a priority for France and created an enduring institutional structure, were of critical importance.[29]

De Gaulle created the institutions that would define France's population policy: a new social security system, the Institut national de la démographie (INED), and, very briefly, a Ministry of Population. The structure and institutions of postwar population policy were established before de Gaulle's departure from government on January 20, 1946, and many key appointments were already made. For example, the INED was established on October 24, 1945, under Alfred Sauvy; the social security system was created in 1945 as well. The Haut comité consultatif de la population remained, but with a more limited role. French population policy was provided with a solid institutional basis.

The development of these institutions fostered long-term population planning. This was possible because of policy consensus, institutional stability, a core of qualified high officials, and adequate resources. As in Sweden, a pronatalist population policy became an essential element of the nascent welfare state and was thoroughly integrated with it. The result was continuity and predictability. Families could make important life choices based on the stability of policies. Family policy was a rare area of political consensus in France and responded to a felt need of the population. Tangible benefits provided to families deepened public support. Family programs gained virtually iconic status.

Because of the pragmatic nature of state policy, French policy has evolved to meet changing needs. French policy moved from a first consensus immediately following World War II based on public support for the "traditional" family—state familialism—to a second consensus, formulated in the 1960s, based on a broader conception of the family, increased focus on sexual equality, and reconciliation of women's role in the workplace and the family. Claude Martin argues that French family policy has been defined around two poles of tension: familialism versus individualism and universality versus selectivity.[30] He defines four main periods in postwar French family policy. The 1945–65 period was the "Golden Age," corresponding with the baby boom, with "strong incentives to promote fertility and compensate for the cost of children via universal and extensive family benefits. Spending for these benefits amounted to half of social security expenditures in the mid-1950s." From 1965 to 1975, the focus shifted to women's rights and emancipation; the period 1975–85 focused on equality and poverty, with the development of means-tested benefits and priority given to disadvantaged families. Since 1985, the focus has been on reconciling work and family: "Confronted with high unemployment levels and pressures to contain spending, family policies became progressively streamlined as an adjunct to employment policy."[31]

The end of the baby boom in the 1960s, growing numbers of women in the labor force, and the rise of feminism required moving away from reliance on the "traditional" family as the means of maintaining replacement-level birth rates. At the same time, financial constraints made it impossible to increase expenditures. This raised the question of relying more on "vertical" redistribution, that is, means testing and targeting.[32]

Why did French family policy evolve from familialism to reconciliation of work and family, such as in Sweden and Scandinavia, rather than continued support for the "traditional" family, as in Italy? Why did France became a leader "in the availability of publicly run or publicly financed child care services—programs that play a crucial role in promoting women's participation in the labor force"?[33] Kimberly Morgan argues effectively that the reason was the triumph of Gaullist statism over Catholic subsidiarity, of modernization over traditionalism.[34] She attributes this to the weakness and ultimate failure of Christian Democracy in France. "The establishment of the French system in the absence of strong Christian Democratic parties reaffirms the finding that such parties have been the driving force behind traditionalist parties in other countries."[35] For a variety of reasons the balance of forces in France favored the development of statist policies.

The histories of the pronatalist movement and the family movement in France were distinct, as they belonged to different political subcultures. Pronatalists, as discussed previously, were concerned with increasing the French population for reasons of national security. In terms of nineteenth-century politics, that movement was republican rather than Catholic, and some of its most conspicuous representatives were anticlerical. The family movement came from the Catholic world, which during the Third Republic had been marginalized and was often antisystem. The Mouvement Républicain Populaire (MRP), the new postwar Christian Democrat party, led by members of the Resistance, played a positive role in incorporating political Catholicism into the democratic political system. To some extent, it achieved the goals of some of its founders in pursuing left-of-center policies with the votes of the right. The MRP helped make family policy a legitimate subject for the Republic. But its influence was constrained. Unlike the Italian Christian Democrats, the MRP was never hegemonic. At its height, it received about one quarter of the vote.

After World War II, there was widespread support for strengthening the traditional family. But familialism in France was predominantly state familialism—as opposed to Church familialism.[36] The traditional family was the *means*, not the *goal*. Afterward, when it became evident that the traditional family was eroding, women were joining the workforce in increasing numbers, and French economic development required female participation, pronatalists were willing to transfer their support to reconciliation of work and family.

De Gaulle supported pronatalism in order to accomplish his goal of restoring French power. His interest in family issues was secondary. He did not have great sympathy for the MRP, which claimed to be his supporter, the so-called party of fidelity, but which he felt sold him out in 1946. The pro-Gaullist Rassemblement pour la France movement created in 1947 returned the favor; it dealt a severe blow to MRP support, and the Union pour la nouvelle République, which had been created to support de Gaulle after his return to power in 1958, provided a coup de grâce to the MRP. Nor did de Gaulle have warm feelings toward the Church, whose hierarchy largely backed the Vichy regime and whose role was compromised (and permanently weakened) by its policies of collaboration. French population policy was set at the time of the Liberation when de Gaulle was president of the Provisional Government; after 1958, de Gaulle and his successor presidents of the Fifth Republic followed statist or socially liberal policies.

One reason that statism triumphed over subsidiarity after World War II was the legacy of previous struggles. As Morgan points out, the battle over who should educate the young was in fact the key policy debate of the late nineteenth and early twentieth centuries, pitting the secular left against the Catholic right. Republicans feared the forces of the antirepublican Catholic right. They believed that control over education would determine whether the democratic republic would consolidate its power. Through the Ferry Laws of the 1880s, the republicans created a secularist public school system in the 1880s and removed the clergy from any role in the public schools. The same process occurred in the realm of child care and early childhood education. Church-run institutions were abolished and the *écoles maternelles* were established under the Ministry of Education to care for a largely working class clientele: "Although the provision was not meant to help women combine child care and waged work, it certainly had that effect."[37]

Thus, the French state was involved in child care early on. After World War II, the *école maternelle* went from being a program for the working class to a universalist program like the Swedish preschool and remains structured in such a way as to facilitate women's employment. It did not provide for most children under three years of age, however. But by extension, there was no reason why the state should not develop programs for younger children.

Public child care expanded from the 1960s on to facilitate female employment. In the early 1970s, Prime Minister Jacques Chaban-Delmas, who supported women's employment as part of his New Society plans, increased funding for public child care, "changing the resolutions governing the *crèches* [i.e., day care centers] to extend these services to less impoverished families, thereby shedding their image as programs for the poor and fostering a constituency of parents who began to regard the provision of public day care as an entitlement."[38] Much of the funding came from the family branch of Social Security. In the 1980s, however, policy changed as the government began to support diversified solutions to child care, including registered child minders and nannies. There were also programs to enable women to take care of children at home.

One reason for finding alternatives to public day care is that they were less expensive than day care centers. The other was the rise of unemployment. Unskilled women could become registered child minders, thereby eliminating a black market in child minders and reducing unemployment. The Allocation parentale d'éducation, instituted in 1985, provided a low-paid leave for women to take care of their own children. It was intended to take low-skilled women out of the workforce to drive down unemployment. The irony of the situation has been pointed out. Working became a phenomenon of middle-class women while poor and less-qualified women were encouraged to stay home.[39] One specificity of the French system is that French mothers with young children tend to work full time, whereas mothers in Sweden are more likely to work part time.[40]

In the 1980s, there was also a new focus on childhood poverty. New means-tested programs were initiated to address issues of poverty and the needs of single parents. French family, demographic, labor force, and social policies are no longer separate, and the number of benefit programs and allowances has multiplied.

French Family Policy Today

French population and family policies are adequately financed, and based on a well-organized and well-funded infrastructure, and they rely on a small cadre of experienced civil servants. According to 2009 statistics from the Organization for Economic Cooperation and Development, France spent about 4 percent of its gross domestic product on family benefits in cash, services, and tax measures. The way spending is counted determines the result, of course, but French spending is certainly on the high end within the EU.[41] But this does not include programs like the *école maternelle*, which is under the Ministry of Education but provides free early childhood education to almost all French children over the age of three years and to some children under three.

The most important institutional base is the so-called family branch of the social security system, the Caisse nationale des allocations familiales (CNAF). Following the creation of the Social Security system in 1945, there was a debate over whether funds for family programs should be included in a unified social welfare system or comprise a separate branch—a debate that was eventually won by the autonomists. This is a very powerful organization because it provides vast amounts of benefits: €68.5 billion in 2008. The family branch is audited and evaluated by the highly professional Inspection générale des affaires sociales (IGAS). As noted above, France boasts a major research institute, the INED. In 2009, the Haut conseil de la population et de la famille was merged with the Conférence de la famille to create the Haut conseil de la famille, the highest-level advisory body, under a distinguished longtime civil servant, Bertrand Fragonard.

There is also a role for the input of family associations. The Union national des associations familiales (UNAF) operated as an advisory association within the CNAF. According to Claude Martin, it exercises little influence on policy.[42] Michel Chauvière goes further: "In welcoming many ideas and representatives into legitimate institutions of the second rank (like the Economic and Social Council), the political power cuts out any risk of opposition on this front. This is a neocorporatist system, since it's the State that has accorded the monopoly of representation of family interests to a single federal organization."[43] But there are limits to the low profile of family associations. In 1998 Prime Minister Lionel Jospin decided to subject *allocations familiales* to means testing, but the decision was reversed a year later. This was one occasion when the UNAF went public, waging a vigorous and successful lobbying effort based on the argument that family policy is not social policy but "a policy of solidarity intended to compensate for the cost of the child."[44]

Similarly, in 2013, attempts to means test family allowances in order to reduce France's budget deficit were defeated by strong popular opposition.

Because of the strong institutional support for family policy and its important role, there has been, in the words of Claude Martin, a small "welfare elite" composed of a few high-level civil servants who also served on ministerial staffs. These officials have been instrumental in shielding family policy from ideas for radical change emanating from the political sphere. For example, on two occasions, the ministers of social affairs, Michèle Barzach and Simone Weil, worked with senior advisers to prevent policy changes based on ideological considerations.[45]

In addition, there is a community of experts who share in the basic consensus about goals, but differ on means. The result is a serious, dense, and often technical dialogue manifested in publications internal and external to the government. The high quality of the discussion means that policy decisions are likely to be made carefully and based on a thorough understanding. The result is stability and coherence:

> Long-lasting policies are necessary in order to maintain people's
> trust and convince them that no profound changes will occur in
> the future. Continuous and diversified policies are also needed
> to guarantee long-term support and create "systemic" coherence.
> The existence of coherent support, balancing benefits in cash
> and kind, and providing continuous support to parents as their
> children grow up is certainly a precondition for effective policies.
> This is a key aspect in explaining France's performance, and
> goes beyond direct financial incentives.[46]

A 2011 publication of the Haut conseil de la population, *Architecture de la politique familiale*, provides an invaluable summary of the goals of French family policy, the means utilized to achieve them, and the state of the debate. What makes this document especially important is that it is semiofficial. According to this report, the two historic goals of French policy on which there is relative consensus are to support natality and to compensate the expenses of the family with children. Supporting natality is "historically one of the explicit objectives of family policy in France," but "family policy today no longer explicitly pursues a natalist objective but aims to support parents in the realization of their desire for children. It is expected that this policy will produce the maintenance of or increase in the birth rate that is as much an end in itself as an indicator of the satisfaction of the wishes of parents, and in so doing, success of the policy followed."[47]

Reconciliation of family and professional life has become the center of governmental policy, which likewise is expected to lead to population increase.[48] This goal contributes to equality between men and women and "consolidates growth and improves the financing of social systems."[49] But there is still some debate between those who support freedom of choice to facilitate the traditional family and those who promote greater equality between the sexes.[50] However, what is a central (and crippling) debate in some countries, such as Italy, is usually a limited conversation among experts in France.

Two other goals involving but not restricted to family policy are contributing to care for young adults and the struggle against poverty. In the former case, the issue is whether the task is incumbent on family policy or other kinds of policy instruments. In the latter case, the main policy tool, the *revenu minimum d'insertion*, although paid through the family branch is not paid by it, and there are still debates over approaches and tools.

French policy is familialist in that it recognizes the existence of the family as an institution that lies between the state and the individual. Familialism "makes of the family—and not just the individual— . . . the reference point of public policies in matters of population, protection, redistribution, employment, citizenship. . . . [It is] the principal mediation between the State and citizens, even constituting a 'democratic' society concurrent to citizen individualism."[51]

But the French version of familialism is very different from the familialism found in Southern Europe, because it is not predicated on the traditional family and does not have a religious dimension.

And because the family is defined in secular, not religious, terms, familialism does not imply reverence for and loyalty to traditional family structures. France thus provides a via media between Northern and Southern societies in Europe (with Germany closer to Southern societies because of its constitutional commitment to protection of the family). In Sweden, the family has ceased to have legal recognition; all benefits and taxes are individualized. In Italy, only the traditional family is recognized and receives benefits. In France, the definition of family has expanded to include all kinds of nontraditional arrangements, including single parents, gay couples with children, and, in many but not all respects, couples joined in civil unions. Thus, France, like Italy, and unlike Sweden, recognizes the legal status of the family, but the spirit and content of French policy is much closer to that of Sweden. And just as in Sweden, about half of the births in France take place out of wedlock. "All differences between the rights of children born inside or outside of marriage have been removed from the law."[52] Broad definition of the family means broad eligibility for benefits and services.

French family policy constitutes a dense web of policies. This is not the place to describe each, but it is important to provide an idea of the range of programs.[53] The oldest program is the *allocations familiales*, which date back to 1939. They provide support for families with at least two children (originally three). Their real value declined from a high point after World War II when the family received 30 percent of the father's salary for the third child. At that time, a "single salary allowance" (*allocation de salaire unique*) was also paid to families in which only the father worked and was higher than the *allocation familiale*.[54] The purpose of this allowance was to keep women out of the workplace and in the home. It was later reduced, then means-tested, and finally abolished in 1978.[55] Today, families with two children receive €125.78 a month; families with three children receive €286.94, with €161.17 for each additional child. Unlike many other countries, France does not provide equal support for each child; larger families continue to get greater support, revealing the pronatalist origins of the policy.

Also dating from 1945 is the *quotient fiscal* (family ratio). This provides tax deductions for parents with children and is separate from the family branch of Social Security. Income tax is reduced based on the size of the family, with increased benefits for families with three or more children. The *quotient* does not benefit those with low incomes, who pay little in the way of taxes; it mostly benefits those who pay high taxes, but there is a ceiling for deductions. There are also tax deductions for external child care and for a home care assistant; in the latter case, 50 percent of expenses of up to €10,000 can be deducted. The poverty rate fell from 21 percent to 7.2 percent as a result of transfers to families with children.[56] Another non-means-tested benefit is maternity leave. Maternity leave begins six weeks before the due date and extends for ten weeks after birth. The stipend is paid through national health insurance. There is also a two-week paternity leave.

According to Olivier Thévenon, low-income and well-off households benefit most from family policies; the "average amount of child-related transfers is U-shaped."[57] He also provides a breakdown on spending (non-income-tax-related): parental leave benefit, 9 percent; maternity/paternity leave, 8 percent; social assistance, 11 percent; state investment in child care and preschool, 3 percent; support for employed home care, 10 percent; family benefits, 53 percent; tax credit for employers, 0.1 percent; and city spending on child care structures, 6 percent. In 2013, it was decided to limit *quotient fiscal* benefits for the well-off in order to maintain family allowances.

There are three competing logics inherent in the family benefit system, all of which have their roots in different concepts of the French republican tradition of equality. Some forms of assistance are based on an "egalitarian logic," which supposes that all families should receive an equal level of aid; this is true of *allocations familiales*. They are fixed grants depending on the number of children. Some benefits are based on "familialist logic"; that is, a family at a given income level with children should live at the same level as a family with the same income without children. That is the logic behind horizontal redistribution. The third logic focuses on reducing social inequality; it involves vertical redistribution from rich to poor.

There are certainly critics of current policies and proponents of change. Supporters of pronatalism can take issue with the declining real value of *allocations familiales* and the increase in aid for the elderly versus aid for children. Those who stress the problem of childhood poverty advocate eliminating or restricting benefits that are not means tested. They argue, for example, that the *quotient fiscal* gives far greater benefits to the rich than the poor. Those who focus on gender equality and reconciliation of women's work and family look askance at generous support for stay-at-home moms. More traditional families feel the opposite.

Mireille Elbaum makes reference to some key tensions within the French system. They include the important role of the *quotient fiscal*, which benefits mostly the rich and poor; the absence of support for the first child; and the fact that the privileged place accorded to the family leads to a neglect of young adults.[58] Jérôme Vignon agrees on the latter point; he predicts great future challenges arising from the impoverishment of young people and the failure of the educational system to orient and otherwise prepare young people for the labor market.[59] Access to jobs has declined; companies don't recruit because of excessive supply. He stated that the next president of France will need to focus on education reform, which in turn will spawn reforms in other areas, such as housing and labor market entry. The same point is made quite emphatically in Timothy Smith's book *France in Crisis*. Smith argues that whereas older workers benefit from full employment, job protection, and generous pensions at a relatively young age, young people, women, and minorities face chronic unemployment, temporary jobs, and endless internships. If the latter succeed in getting a job, it comes fairly late, delaying their entry into a settled family life and, presumably, having children. Those born in the 1970s are twice as likely to experience downward social mobility than those born from 1920 to 1950.[60] The gap between insiders and outsiders has parallels in Italy and therefore should set off alarm bells. On the other hand, children leave home at an age near the European average, and the housing market does not prevent them from doing so.[61]

There has been a long debate about whether family benefits should be means tested and whether the system should be more targeted. In a frequently cited article, Julien Damon traces the debate and argues against such an approach, which in his opinion goes against the original objectives of Social Security. It also can be a pretext for cutting government spending: "In a period of tension, indeed, of budgetary crisis, some may suggest the selectivity of allowances, in order, certainly, to help the most disadvantaged, but above all, to reduce social spending."[62] Targeting can be intended either to "complete the insurance mechanisms and universal allowances, or to replace them, partially or totally."[63] The poor, however, benefit most from a system of universal allowances. Damon argues that targeting results in perverse consequences, including stigmatizing the very population whose particularities the policies are meant to eliminate, and the creation of a split between those who benefit and those who do not that results in reduced support for the programs. Making family and population policy part of social policy means that the criteria for defining funding programs will no longer be based on criteria specific to family and population.

There is strong philosophical grounding for each of the above approaches as well as practical arguments against any given program. But the coexistence of diverse approaches to family support necessarily leads to continual debate about a possible modification of the system, especially as economic, social, and financial conditions evolve. It is impossible to establish a hierarchy of these three concepts of equality. Strong constituencies and interest groups resist change. In addition, policymakers realize the importance of continuity and predictability of policy. The long-term trend has been toward increasing means-tested programs (from 13.5 percent in 1970 to 60 percent in the 1990s). Nevertheless, the very existence of a reasoned debate between competing logics can be seen as a strength of the French system.

A French Success Story

France today experiences "high and stable fertility."[64] The average woman has about two children. This represents a fundamental change in French demography since the nineteenth century. "Still a minority on the eve of the Revolution, Malthusian couples became the majority before the middle of the 19th century, and progressively, voluntary limitation tended to become a general phenomena. . . . Numerous families became more and more rare and it is probable that they were more and more perceived as marginal. However, they were the ones who assured the greatest part of the descendents of a generation. . . . As late as 1906, 30 percent of couples were responsible for almost 57 percent of babies."[65]

Today, the average age of mothers at the first birth has increased but so has fertility of those in their thirties. Laurent Toulemon points out that "the case of France invalidates the two most commonly held explanations of low fertility: . . . Delay in entry into parenthood . . . [and] the breakdown of traditional family forms." He attributes "France's relatively high fertility" to its "particularly active family policy."[66]

The baby boom and immigration resulted in a significant increase in the French population in the decades following World War II. In fact, the relative population growth between 1950 and 1988 was twice that of the 1850–1950 period.[67] Even though birth rates fell somewhat afterward, they remain fairly high. The French population today is therefore about 50 percent greater than in the late nineteenth century and interwar period and continues to increase. Although immigration has contributed to French population growth, contrary to what many people believe, "immigrants' daughters born in France have exactly the same total fertility as women born in France to mothers themselves born in France."[68]

Péguy once said, after the conclusion of the Dreyfus Affair, that "*tout commence en mystique et finit en politique*" (everything begins with mystique and ends up in politics). Pronatalism began as mystique in France but was then successfully incorporated into the welfare state. The development of a consensus to support the family as it evolved from traditional to nontraditional forms and the reconciliation of work and children has largely resolved the dilemma of France's low birth rate and made French people happier, more secure, and more egalitarian. The current birth rate also means a reasonable dependency ratio in the future, which will make it easier for France to maintain the very welfare state whose existence perpetuates its relatively high birth rate. Because the French system provides a wide variety of support to many forms of families and is less ideological than the Swedish, it may be a better model for low-birth-rate countries.

CHAPTER THREE

Italy: The Absence of Policy

Fascist social policies would long remain (and still remain) the only systematic family policy that Italy has ever known.

—MANUELA NALDINI[1]

It is not radical revolution, . . . which is a Utopian dream for Germany, but rather a partial, merely political revolution, which leaves the pillars of the building standing.

—KARL MARX[2]

ITALY'S LOWEST LOW BIRTH RATE has put the future of the nation at risk; thanks to a huge proportion of old people and a declining number of children, the Italian population pyramid is top heavy. Italy is one of the oldest countries in the world, and the native Italian population is already in decline. Yet little has been done to resolve or even mitigate the problem. Unlike Sweden and France, whose governments responded effectively to sagging birth rates and helped reverse the trend, Italy's weak and divisive political system is part of the problem, rather than part of the solution. Explaining why the Italian state has failed may help explain why other states (especially those in Southern Europe) have also been ineffective.

In this chapter, I first examine Italy's demographic situation, then summarize current family policies, go on to inquire why the Italian birth rate is so low, and, finally, analyze state policy.

Italy's Demography

The Italian population is aging and declining. The demographic history of Italy in the last thirty years is one of continued decline of the birth rate followed by stabilization at a lowest-low level: "The period total fertility rate (PTFR) fell below 2 children in 1977, below 1.5 in 1984, and below 1.3 in 1993. In the following decade, the PTFR was relatively stable around 1.25."[3] These birth rates are not radically different from those of other countries in Southern or Germanic Europe but are far lower than those of Northern Europe and France. Regional differences within Italy (the South used to have a higher birth rate than the North) have become less marked.

Ten years ago, the demographer Peter McDonald addressed what it would take to stabilize Italy's population. McDonald argued that the Italian population would remain roughly stable under the following scenarios: a TFR constant at 1.2, with an immigration rate rising to 400,000 per year; a TFR rising to 1.6, with immigration at 200,000 per year; and a TFR rising to 1.8, with immigration at 100,000.[4] At present, Italy's demography approximates McDonald's extreme case of a low birth rate along with high immigration.

The eminent demographer Massimo Livi-Bacci states that "under the current biodemographic profile, the current fertility rate implies the halving of the Italian population every forty years. Thirty years from now, women over eighty would be more numerous than girls under puberty, and those over seventy would exceed those below thirty."[5] The dependency ratio would become extremely problematic, as a decreasing number of working adults would be called on to support a growing number of senior citizens.

Current Policies

Italian policies in support of the family are extremely limited and fragmented. Italy spends a small percentage of what France and Sweden devote to family policy. According to the Organization for Economic Cooperation and Development, France spends 3.7 percent of its gross domestic product (GDP) on family benefits in cash, services, and tax measures; Sweden, 3.1; and Italy, 1.4. As for spending on maternity and parental leave payments per child, Sweden spends 59 percent of its per capita GDP; France, 28 percent; and

Italy, 18 percent. Italy provides robust support for families in only two areas: maternity leave and early childhood education.

There is compulsory maternity leave for five months at 80 percent of salary. The program was considered advanced when it was established in 1971. It was extended to a wider category of women (originally it included only the employed), but its duration has not been increased. Paid paternity leave does not exist, except for single fathers and fathers with ill spouses. In addition, there is parental leave for up to six months per parent until the child is eight years of age, paid at 30 percent.

The problem of maternity leave is that its benefits do not extend to those employed under flexible contracts, which include a large percentage of the young and female population—in short, those likely to be mothers. Many workers under flexible contracts (*contratto a tempo determinato*, or *precario*) are expected to sign a *dimissioni in bianco*, an undated letter of resignation that means they can be dismissed at will by the employer—for example, in the event of pregnancy. This practice was banned by the Prodi government of 2006–8, but was reinstated by the Berlusconi government in 2008.

The other major service provided by the Italian state is the *scuola maternal,* early childhood education for children beginning at the age of three years, which, like the *école maternelle* in France, most children attend. Strictly speaking, this program is not considered a social service but rather education. It is under the Ministry of Education and employs regular qualified teachers.

Other benefits, like family allowances, have ceased to be very significant. The family allowance was instituted under fascism to create a "family wage." It provided a significant supplement to a worker's wages for each dependent child. Under the Republic, the cash value of the allowance was held steady, so that its real value decreased. It is now a means-tested program that applies only to the poor. There is a great deal of talk about initiating a *quotient fiscal* like that of France, but as of this writing, nothing had been accomplished. The Prodi government initiated a baby bonus that would have provided tax benefits for two years (probably too short a period to make much of a difference), but the subsequent Berlusconi government cut the benefits to one year and then eliminated them completely. The entire program survived only eighteen months. Yet the effects of such programs require continuity and predictability.

There is also a lack of adequate preschool for children under three. But it is not clear whether the problem is one of supply or demand. "The lack of public services offering child care is partly due to low demand for these services owing to a strong cultural bias against the practice to send the smallest children outside the home."[6] Conversely, lack of quality public child care in some regions must also reduce demand.

What is striking is the huge gap between spending for the elderly versus spending for children in Italy. The elderly-child ratio is 5.3:1 (compared with 1:2 in Sweden).[7] An index compiled by Julia Lynch shows Sweden spending 22.9 percent of its per capita GDP on children under fifteen; France, 12.9; and Italy, 5.46. Spending on the elderly is, respectively, 62.3, 84.1, and 90.4 percent of per capita GDP.[8]

Familialism

Italy suffers from a negative synergy between family and state. The paradox is that the decline in the Italian birth rate arises not from the weakness of the traditional family but from its continued strength. The family continues to perform a wide range of social welfare roles that elsewhere are performed by the state (although increasingly care of the elderly is performed in the home by immigrants). The result is that public institutions remain weak, underdeveloped, and often ineffectual. The fecklessness of the state in turn becomes a rationalization for continued minimization of its role. As some Italians have asserted in conversations with the author, Italian voters have elected and sustained a government that epitomizes—and justifies—their own lack of faith in state institutions.

Edward Banfield's 1958 book *The Moral Basis of a Backward Society*, which is focused on a small town in the South, popularized the concept of "amoral familism." The author believed that this phenomenon underlay the community's social behavior (he did not claim that it applied to Italy as a whole): "Maximize the material, short-term advantage of the nuclear family; assume that all others will do likewise."[9] Although Banfield has been roundly attacked by social scientists for some of his later work, "amoral familism" seems to retain some cachet in Italy as a metaphor for the lack of respect for civic institutions and civic culture. The Italian would be like Rigoletto, deeply devoted to his family whom he tries to protect against a hostile outside world but feeling no loyalty to others; in fact, he makes his living by mocking others, in this way contributing to the world's corruption.

Italians have little trust in those outside of kin relations. "Another important consequence of Italian familism—and the low esteem of civic values—is the gap between private wealth and the quality of public services."[10] Most welfare expenditures are directly transferred from the state to families, rather than to public services.[11] Social scientists frequently refer to David Reher's seminal article to help explain the historical origins and role of familialism in Italy.[12]

The existence of such strong familialism undermines social reform. The family constitutes a welfare system that protects young people from unemployment and enables them to refuse substandard jobs, reducing social pressure on the government to address chronic unemployment. By providing free housing for thirty-year-olds in the family home, it weakens the impetus to create an affordable rental sector. It cushions the impact of a dual-track employment system in which young people (as well as women and minorities) suffer precarious employment with few benefits. (Who has not been astounded by the extremely high unemployment figures for young people in Southern Europe even before the Great Recession?) At the same time, the burden of caring for the elderly falls mostly on middle-aged and not-so-middle-aged children. The result is a family strategy of husbanding resources for one or two children. Note that this common strategy was employed in nineteenth-century France and contemporary China to achieve upward social mobility. But here one suspects it is being used to prevent downward mobility. By the time these children emerge into the adult world, they are often in their thirties and have little experience in living on their own or with contemporaries. Young men expect to be taken care of rather than to contribute to housework. This makes the idea of marriage and children less attractive to women who have a successful career. Marriage comes late, and there is little time to have more than a few children.

As Massimo Livi-Bacci writes, "Reproductive decisions appear as the final result of a series of steps that have to be taken in sequence." He cites "the gradual postponement, among recent generations, of the age at which education is completed, the labor market is entered, a stable job is found, a home is selected, the family is left, a partnership is initiated. Each step is a condition for the successive one."[13]

Gianpiero Dalla Zuanna states that "the strategy of reducing fertility has been a good familistic tool in Italy over the last 30 years, helping the social climb of few children or the only child."[14] He concludes: "But the persistence of a familistic society could be a pyrrhic victory, because—if fertility does not substantially increase—the native population risks rapid aging and decline."[15] Presumably, the burden on the family could become too great. Can a single wage earner support wife, children, and aging parents? What if he does not have a standard labor contract? Especially at a time of economic crisis, the family could buckle under its economic burden. If workers get old without benefits, the Italian family can implode.

Familialism is at least as much a consequence of state failure as the cause of economic and social crisis. The greatest problem facing Italians is decent employment—permanent, well-paying jobs with access to benefits. It was frequently argued that high unemployment in Italy was the result of rigid regulation. The center-left government (not the Berlusconi government), with the cooperation of the trade unions, "reformed" the system in such a way that older workers retained benefits and security whereas younger workers and those just entering the job market were forced into "nonstandard" jobs, such as part-time and fixed-term employment.

"The majority of these workers are enjoying fewer welfare entitlements than people employed on a standard full-time contract, including little—if any—income protection in case of dismissal, and no employment protection."[16] Nor have these reforms proven effective against unemployment.

The tragic fate of highly educated young Italians—suffering from unemployment, years in poorly paid temporary jobs, or unpaid internships—is no secret:

> Francesca Esposito, 29 and exquisitely educated, helped win millions of euros in false disability and other lawsuits for her employer, a major Italian state agency. But one day last fall she quit, fed up with how surreal and ultimately sad it is to be young in Italy today. It galled her that even with her competence and fluency in five languages, it was nearly impossible to land a paying job. Working as an unpaid trainee lawyer was bad enough, she thought, but doing it at Italy's social security administration seemed too much. She not only worked for free on behalf of the nation's elderly, who have generally crowded out the young for jobs, but her efforts there did not even apply to her own pension. "It was absurd," said Ms. Esposito, a strong-willed woman with a healthy sense of outrage.[17]

In most advanced societies today, there is a correlation between the percentage of women working and higher birth rates. In Italy, the percentage of working women is one of the lowest. Society and the state do little to facilitate the reconciliation of work and family. Social mores still tend to condemn women for not staying home with young children. Mothers do not feel comfortable with child care, whose quality and nature varies throughout the country because it is a regional and local responsibility rather than a federal one. Because school hours do not correspond with work hours, it is difficult to combine part-time work with family. Nor is part-time work common: "There is strong evidence that women's birth strike is caused by employer unwillingness to introduce flexible working hours, and to employ or re-employ pregnant women or those who are mothers."[18] So women must basically choose between children or career. Not surprisingly, the number of childless women has risen for decades, especially in the North. For the cohort of 1960, "women with two children (37.2 percent) are outnumbered by the sum of mothers of an only child (20.5 percent) and of childless women (24.2 percent)."[19]

De Rose points out that Italy's extraordinarily low birth rates are not the result of the revolution in contraceptives. In 1996, for instance, 34 percent of married women and 12 percent of nonmarried women relied on coitus interruptus, and condoms and withdrawal were still more popular than the pill![20]

The survival of the "traditional family" has another consequence. Nontraditional relationships, like cohabitation, are less common in Italy (and less accepted) than in France and Sweden. Few children are born out of wedlock. Yet it seems that in Europe higher birth rates are tied to a higher percentage of out-of-wedlock births.

In Italy, there is a huge gap between the interest of the individual and the interests of society. But it is not the task of the individual or the family to sacrifice immediate interests to a hypothetical national interest. As we have seen, pronatalists in late-nineteenth-century and early-twentieth-century France utterly failed to increase birth rates by exhortation (not that there is much of that in Italy today). It is the task of the political system to develop alternate long-term policies to reconcile individual and family interests with social interests. That is what governments did in Sweden and France. That is precisely what is lacking in Italy.

An Ineffective State

The causes for the failure to develop an effective Italian state policy response to low birth rates are overdetermined. It is as if all the stars are aligned against Italy. In this section, I examine the factors that have negated development of effective policy.

One important reason for the failure of the postwar Italian state to develop an effective policy response to declining birth rates was the reaction against fascist pronatalism. The pronatalist goals of fascist policy were gratuitous and even absurd; Italian birth rates had long been too high, and Italy was a major source of emigration. Some of the means employed, however, especially family allowances and health care, were beneficial. The postwar Republic marked a discontinuity with fascism's pronatalist goals but also weakened policies that actually helped women. This is not because the Republic systematically reversed all of fascism's policies—far from it—but because of opposition to state familialism.

In the period following the unification of Italy, there was no demographic policy and little family policy. Italy was a liberal state based on the concept of limited government (although the role of the state did expand under Giolitti in the late nineteenth and early twentieth centuries), and the family was not conceived as a subject for state policy. Italy was a relatively poor country and could not afford expensive social programs. It was also a Catholic country where the Church "defended" the family as its privileged domain and opposed state intrusion.

The demographic transition took place in Italy in the late nineteenth century. Mortality rates declined but birth rates remained relatively high. Industrialization was not intense and rapid, so that Italy produced more people than its economy could absorb. There was migration from the South to the industrial North, but also massive emigration, much of it to North and South America. Emigration was the great safety valve to avoid overpopulation; in this respect, Italy was similar to Sweden and unlike France. Emigration could resolve Italy's problem of surplus population because of rapid economic expansion in North and South America.

World War I produced high casualties, and the Italian birth rate declined in the postwar period. Nonetheless, it would have been hard to argue that Italy needed more people rather than fewer. For reasons that were ideological and perhaps psychological (the Duce's overblown sense of his own virility), Mussolini concluded that Italy should pursue a pronatalist policy.[21] This policy was the only coherent population policy Italy ever pursued, but it was wrongheaded and its ends irrational. The context of this policy was the series of fascist "battles" aimed at modernizing Italy, or at least giving the impression of modernizing Italy.

One element of Mussolini's policy was to prevent emigration of Italians abroad, based on the belief that emigration weakened the nation. Perhaps this was an alibi for the humiliatingly low quota placed on the entry of Italian immigrants by the United States. Migration would be regulated by the state, and migrants would be directed to the empire (such as it was) and to what were deemed underpopulated rural areas of Italy; otherwise, the migration would probably have continued from rural areas of the South to urban areas of the North. The second element of fascist policy was to encourage an even higher birth rate. Fascism instituted policies such as prohibitions of contraception and disincentives such as higher taxes for adult unmarried men and, after 1938, the requirement that men be married or widowers for eligibility to enter high-level positions like mayor and university professor. Incentives included reduced income and inheritance taxes for large families and preference in public employment to married men with children.

Some of the means that the fascist government employed in its quixotic quest to raise birth rates were beneficial. Most important was the introduction of family allowances and bonuses at the birth of children. Family allowances were inspired by the notion of the family wage to enable the male head of a family to support his entire family without the need for women to work. This, however, was not an economic possibility. The family allowance provided benefits for all dependents with a low income—including wives, children, parents, and in-laws. There were also low-interest loans for couples that were progressively reduced at the birth of each child and expunged at the birth of the fourth child.[22] The creation of the Opera Nazionale Maternità e Infanzia provided prenatal and postnatal care but also "could supervise and control how women approached their motherhood duties."[23] There is no doubt that these economic and medical benefits were helpful to the average Italian.

In this area, as in many others, the content of fascist policies was close to those advocated by the Church, which also wanted to support the "traditional family." Meanwhile, there was a turf battle between Church and state over who would control the institutions that applied the policies. After all, both the fascist regime and the Church had a totalitarian vision and both wanted to control the family. The Church was the one rival institution that fascism could not throttle. The Lateran Accords of 1929 were in some ways more a truce than a peace settlement; the two institutions would coexist but also compete. It is no surprise that after the fall of fascism, the Church seized the opportunity to push back state intrusion into family policy. Pronatalist policy was now equated to fascism. Republican Italy dismantled some of fascism's pronatalism policies or allowed them to atrophy. The experience of fascism became a justification (or an alibi) for the failure of the Republic to support families with children even when the birth rate fell below replacement level.

ABSENCE OF A POSTWAR PARADIGM SHIFT

According to Chiara Saraceno, "the social policies for the family in our country are reluctant and ambivalent above all because they are the result of an absence."[24] An account of family policy in postwar Italy is more a history of debates and grandstanding than of legislative accomplishments.

Unlike Sweden and France, postfascist Italy never experienced a great period of paradigm shift. Since the fall of fascism, there have been several moments of Italian renewal, but even when added together they do not constitute a change as substantial as that experienced by Sweden in the 1930s or France just after World War II. The first occurred after World War II, when the Republic and democratic political institutions were created. But the internalization of the

Cold War into Italian politics limited change. The second was the short-lived "opening to the left" in the early 1960s with the entry of the Socialist Party into government, which focused on political issues. The third was the spate of socioeconomic reforms of the 1970s around the time of the debate over the "historic compromise." And the fourth was the birth of the "Second Republic" after the implosion of Christian Democracy at the end of the Cold War. Each of these periods of renewal proved disappointing, and the fourth perhaps the most disappointing of all. Only the third produced significant reforms of family policy and social services for women, but because Italy still had a high birth rate, they were unrelated to demographic concerns.

The third period of reform was tied to the increased militancy of the women's movement. The main fruits of this period included legalization of divorce and abortion enacted by Parliament and approved by referenda. In addition, limited but highly significant social and educational programs were introduced, such as the *scuola maternal*, compulsory and paid maternity leave, and some provisions for child care aimed at the very young (birth to three years).

THE PERSISTENCE OF HIGH BIRTH RATES
INTO THE POSTWAR PERIOD

For at least three decades after World War II, Italy had no population policy because it did not have a population problem. The founders of Italy's postwar paradigm did not need to factor into their thinking concerns about population. Nor did demographers foresee the problem of an excessively low birth rate.

In the early 1970s, Massimo Livi-Bacci contributed a chapter to Bernard Berelson's *Population Policy in Developed Countries*. His chapter constitutes an invaluable snapshot of how Italy's demographic situation appeared to trained eyes at that time. Livi-Bacci's abstract at the beginning of his chapter summarizes Italy's principal demographic problems:

(1) a decreasing but still considerable emigration; (2) a moderate level of fertility, which is the result of very different regional fertility levels, too high in the south and too low in the north; (3) differentials in mortality; [and] (4) a very intense process of internal migration under the pressures of rapid economic and social change and of regional differentials—especially in the recent past—of the rates of population growth.[25]

Livi-Bacci states that there was no sense in public debate that policy could influence population:

> Whether as a reaction to the negative experience of the Fascist policy or as a result of the heavy influence of the Catholic morality (unfavorable to family planning), the fact is that never, or at least never significantly since the end of war, has the population growth issue been contemplated.[26]

When, suddenly and unexpectedly, Italy's birth rate fell below replacement level in the late 1970s, and the issue became one of increasing the rate rather than reducing it, the reluctance of the state to become involved in population policy and the Church's opposition to state intrusion hindered the development of family policy. It also took time to recognize that subreplacement or even lowest-low birth rates were not just temporary, but long-term phenomena. In fact, it has been argued that the idea that Italy is by nature a country of high birth rates continues to influence opinion and constitutes an impediment to a pronatalist policy.[27] Some believed that Italy was overpopulated and a lower population was not a bad thing. According to Livi-Bacci, the reality of population decline and its implications did not become clear until the Dini government embarked on pension reform in the 1990s.[28] Thus, the realization that the Italian birth rate had fallen to lowest-low levels for what appeared to be an indefinite period—and that such a decline could have significant implications for the health of the nation—did not occur until late in the postwar period.

With effective family policies—and a greater focus on the needs of women, especially female workers—the decline of Italian birth rates might not have been so precipitous. But such policies were not developed because of a lack of political consensus. In this regard, the situation in Italy differed greatly from that of Sweden and France.

In Sweden, the ideological point of view of the Social Democratic Workers' Party, based on the earner-carer model, became hegemonic. The other political parties basically accepted the Social Democrats' programs. The dominant church, which was Lutheran, neither opposed these programs nor sought to retain an area of privileged institutional control over the family. In France, population policies were focused on pronatalism. But the means to achieve this end were eclectic. French policymakers initially tried to create conditions whereby mothers could remain at home and later instituted social services making it possible to reconcile work with family. As discussed above, although familialism played an important role in family policy after World War II, the role of the Church was marginalized and the political career of Christian Democracy was ephemeral.

The situation was quite different in Italy, where Christian Democracy was the dominant party in Italy from 1946 until the early 1990s. Italian politics was divided into Catholic and secular worlds. Until the end of the Cold War, the Catholic world was represented by the Christian Democratic Party, which was closely tied to the Vatican and headed every Italian government until 1981. The secular world was divided into Marxist and non-Marxist political groupings. The Italian Communist Party (Partito Comunista Italiana, PCI) gained dominance in the Marxist subculture, whereas the non-communist secular parties were relatively small and weak. The Socialist Party was initially allied with the PCI and then split with the party in the late 1950s. In practice, the Christian Democrats and the PCI dominated the political landscape. Their worldviews were largely antithetical.

For the thirty years following World War II, the PCI sought to expand its political base and gain a majority in Parliament in alliance with some of the secularist parties. After 1973, influenced by the coup against Salvador Allende in Chile, the PCI sought a "historic compromise" with the Christian Democrats. Of course, the Cold War and internal Italian politics were intertwined. The United States and its allies feared Communist dominance in Italy and had attempted to prevent the party's electoral victory in 1946 and after; the PCI championed the idea of Eurocommunism to assert the party's democratic bona fides and differentiate it from Soviet-style communism.

Fundamental differences divided the left and right, or secularists and Catholics, on women and the family. The Church wanted to preserve and strengthen the "traditional family" under the dominance of the paterfamilias. Women were supposed to fulfill their historic role as mothers and housewives. Where women had to work out of economic necessity, specific measures could be tailored to help them. The Church strove to maintain its influence over the family and to provide its own services rather than to permit the development of public services in order to maintain a political space for itself. "In Italy, protecting the family meant essentially resisting transformations taking place in the way in which men and women chose to manage their sexual, reproductive and emotional lives."[29]

The left's views were close to those of the Swedish Social Democrats. The left focused on women's individual rights and autonomy. Women should be able to combine work and family; the state should provide social services that enable women to do so. The secularist camp, however, was weakened by the PCI's reluctance to support measures on family issues that might antagonize potential support from traditional Catholic voters—voters they hoped to win over.

The result was much debate over family issues and few legislative accomplishments. On occasions when convergence among parties was achieved, the result was likely to be a watered-down bill that tilted in the direction of familialism. For example, public day care (*nidi*) for the children of working mothers was defined as temporary and custodial rather than an educational service:[30]

> The very complex division of responsibility between the state, the regions, and the local authorities in financing, organizing and running public day care centers limited successful implementation of the law. The initial expectations and purpose of the *nidi* law—to cover 5 percent of children in five years—was not achieved until twenty years after its introduction.[31]

Hot-button issues like divorce, abortion, and assisted reproduction fanned the flames of Italy's culture wars, to the detriment of concrete legislation.[32] As Chiara Sarceno points out, in the 1980s "family questions continued in fact to have low priority in the process of political negotiations, despite their high symbolic character."[33]

In the 1970s, there was a brief moment in which some cooperation between left and right occurred, between the PCI's call for a "historic compromise" in 1974 and Aldo Moro's kidnapping and assassination in 1978. Grassroots demands for change, the rise of the feminist movement, and greater independence of the labor unions helped force the hands of the parties. The assassination of Moro brought this period of limited cooperation to a close. It is important to note that none of this legislation took into account the problem of low birth rates, because Italy was still above replacement level at this time.

It might be imagined that the end of the postwar Italian political system—the collapse of the Christian Democratic Party and Socialist parties and the transformation of the PCI—might have improved the chances for family policy, especially following the end of the Cold War when the problem of demographic decline became manifest. But the conflict between Catholic and secular worldviews then took place within each of the two heterogeneous party coalitions that have governed Italy under the "Second Republic." Some think that the Vatican's influence has actually increased because it can work on both sides of the aisle and its wishes are no longer filtered through the Christian Democrats. As Saraceno pointed out in 1998, the very nature of these party coalitions demonstrated the low priority of family issues. As of this writing, significant policy responses to declining population are still lacking.[34]

THE PROBLEM OF FEDERALISM

Most services relevant to the family, especially health care services, are provided by regional governments. But the role and financial base of the regions have been caught up in the maelstrom of debate, constitutional revisions, and legislation pertaining to federalism and fiscal federalism.[35] The development of the European Union as a supranational entity has been accompanied by an increasing role for subnational units in much of Europe on both levels. The issue of constitutional reform has been particularly problematic in Italy, however, because of its politicization.

The rise of the Northern League, a party that has oscillated between advocacy of decentralization and separatism, has radicalized the debate. Because of the party's control over much of Northern Italy and its indispensable place in the Berlusconi coalition, its views could not be ignored. Yet many of these views were not shared by coalition partners, let alone the opposition. The governing coalition included representation from Sicily, for example, which benefits the most from a unitary state because of large transfers of money from North to South via Rome. That is precisely what the Northern League claimed that it wanted to end. The left, with its focus on equity and solidarity, was also reluctant to accept significant federal reforms, especially where they might result in unequal services. Conversely, because the left wanted to hold on to electoral support in the North, where federalism is popular, it had to at least pay lip service to the concept. Two constitutional reforms passed through a divided Parliament. In 2000 and 2001, one of these survived a referendum, while the other in 2006 did not. Of course, once passed, constitutional measures have to be complemented by enabling legislation, which became another complex and never-ending battleground. Finally, decisions have to be made about financing regional government. Although it is popular to talk about fiscal federalism, there is little agreement about what it should mean in practice. How much of regional funding should derive from sharing of national revenues? How much authority should be granted to regions to create their own tax base? In practice, the federal government always has to bail out the regions.

The point is that the development of programs to support families and children, much of which takes place on the regional level, is necessarily a victim of the incoherence and political infighting that has dominated Italian regional reform for over a decade and seems unlikely to end in the foreseeable future. It is another example of too much politics and too little policymaking.

ECONOMIC AND FINANCIAL PROBLEMS

In the words of the *Economist*'s *Country Report Italy*, long-term economic problems stem from the following factors:

> low productivity; high unit labour costs relative to the country's main trading partners; specialisation in low- and medium-technology manufacturing sectors competing directly with products from countries with lower labour costs; weak competition in non-tradable services; and the predominance of small- and medium-sized enterprises, . . . which need to expand and invest in innovation and research and development.[36]

Italy's long-term, chronic problems would be hard to resolve under the best of conditions, but slow recovery throughout the West from the global recession and Italy's dysfunctional political system make improvements in the foreseeable future hard to imagine. Greater spending by the Italian government is precluded by the extremely high level of national debt (about 120 percent of GDP).

Italy faces a truly dreary economic and financial situation, dominated by the euro crisis, a result of slow growth, weak competitiveness, high debt, and high deficits. Italy's membership in the euro zone prevented it from engaging in its traditional remedy: competitive devaluation. Instead, the threat of being caught up in the euro crisis resulted in very tight control over expenditures toward the end of the Berlusconi period, to the detriment of the country's economic recovery. The Monti government placed Italy in survival mode. Its goal was to prevent the country from being forced into a bailout and to keep it in the euro zone—and to prevent a collapse of the euro zone itself.

The consequences for dealing with Italy's demographic problems are huge. First, dire financial straits make it difficult to imagine the creation of any major new social service programs that could help women reconcile work and family. There is no way that Italy could contemplate raising expenditures to support children to the level of France or Sweden, which would involve more than doubling Italy's spending to at least 3 percent of GDP. Second, Italy's competitiveness problem will perpetuate precarious forms of employment that exclude social benefits to keep labor costs down. That, in turn, will depress birth rates. The emphasis will remain on short-term solutions rather than long-term change. Birth rates cannot improve as long as young Italians lack access to long-term job security and a dynamic labor market.

One way that Italy has dealt with labor shortages, especially low-skilled labor, is through immigration. In 2011, net migration into Italy was 4.86 per 1,000 population, three times that of France and Sweden and about the same as Singapore.[37] As of January 1, 2002, the foreign population in Italy was 1,3546,590. Nine years later, it was 4,570,317.[38] According to the Organization for Economic Cooperation and Development, the proportion of foreign-born residents in Italy grew from 2.5 percent in 2001 to 5.8 percent in 2007.[39] That is to say that the foreign-born population grew about 2 million in six years, close to what Peter McDonald estimated was needed to maintain a stable population with a TFR of 1.2. Not surprisingly, this high level of immigration has been grist for the mill of the Northern League, a right-wing, xenophobic, demagogic party that is the governing party but behaves like an opposition party.

Illegal female immigrants have played an especially important role in caring for Italy's burgeoning elderly population. They have helped to replace family members as caretakers of elders but have enabled the elderly to remain at home. They have also reduced the need for professional care and social services. Periodic regularization of their status has encouraged continued immigration.[40]

Short of an unanticipated tectonic change in the Italian birth rate, the nation is set for one of two tragic fates: either a long-term decline in population, which will threaten Italy's survival as a prosperous, advanced economy; or a solution to the demographic problem through tolerance of large-scale but barely controlled immigration, which could threaten public order, polarize the nation politically, and exceed Italy's capacity to integrate newcomers. In either case, Italy's vital interests would be threatened.

CHAPTER FOUR

Japan: The Politics
of Position Taking

No amount of well-meaning policy statements on gender can off-
set the impact of dwindling income and mounting job insecurity
on people's willingness to have bigger families.

—OSAWA MARI[1]

THE JAPANESE BIRTH RATE fell below replacement levels in 1974 and has continued to sink. In concrete terms, the figures are startling. The number of births fell from 2,670,000 in 1974 to 1,760,000 in 2002; the number of households with children went from 53 percent in 1975 to 28.2 percent in 2003.[2] Since 2005, the nation's total population has been in decline. Japan's National Institute of Population and Social Security Research shows continuing population decline to 100.6 million in 2050 (Japan's population in 2000 was about 127 million); long-range projections indicate that population will drop even faster afterward.[3]

At the same time, Japan's population has been aging rapidly and is now the oldest in the world. In 2000, 17.4 percent of the population was over sixty-five years of age; in 2014, 25 percent will be over sixty-five; in 2050 it is estimated that 35.7 percent will be over sixty-five, that is, 1 in 2.8 persons.[4] The noted demographer Nicholas Eberstadt describes Japan's postwar decline in fertility as a "virtual collapse" and writes that "gradually but relentlessly, Japan is evolving into a type of society whose contours and workings have only been contemplated in science fiction."[5] Immigration, which might help mitigate the birth rate decline, is politically unacceptable. The contrast between the magnitude of the threat to Japan's national survival posed by low birth rates and declining population and the inadequacy of the policy response is striking.

The decline in the birth rate is not the only crisis facing Japan. After defeat in World War II, which marked the end of a period of imperialism in Asia, Japan reinvented itself as one of the world's great industrial nations. It seemed to have developed a unique formula for economic expansion. Japan appeared to be winning in economic competition what it had failed to win in war. In the 1980s, Japan's growth challenged American economic supremacy. A school of "declinist" literature emerged in the United States, purporting to explain Japanese success and American failure. In the 1990s, however, the Japanese economic model sputtered and stalled. Economic growth has never recovered, nor have public finances. The national debt is now the largest of any developed nation, over 220 percent of gross national product. In 2010, Japan lost its place as the world's second-largest economy to China. The Fukushima nuclear disaster of 2011 raised doubts about the security of Japan's nuclear energy programs, the credibility of Japan's private sector, and the integrity of government oversight. Political gridlock has accompanied economic failure: when the voters finally ousted the long-ruling Liberal Democrats in 2009, the winning Democratic Party of Japan turned out to be equally factionalized and ineffective. How did a nation that was so successful in the first three decades of the postwar era become incapable of reforming itself?

The Fertility Crisis

Japanese women say they want to marry and have children, but in practice they are increasingly reluctant. There is a huge gap between the desired number of children and the number who are actually born. The root of Japan's problem of low fertility is nicely encapsulated in the quotation by Peter McDonald cited in earlier chapters:

> Very low fertility is the product of the combination of high gender equity in individual-oriented institutions with the persistence

of only moderate gender equity in family-oriented institutions.
... If women are provided with opportunities near to equivalent
to those of men in education and market employment, but these
opportunities are severely curtailed by having children, then, on
average, women will restrict the number of children that they
have to an extent which leaves fertility at a very low, long-term
level.[6]

Perhaps in Japan we are talking about the gap between medium
gender equity in some individual-oriented institutions, such as big
business, and high in others, such as education, and low gender
equity in family-oriented institutions.

According to Leonard Schoppa's *Race for the Exits*, postwar
Japan developed a highly successful model of "convoy capitalism."
In socioeconomic terms, it involved lifetime employment, managed
competition, and financial regulation that provided to Japanese
business a "predictable business environment in which they could
make long-term relational commitments to workers, suppliers, and
distributors."[7] These policies were matched by family policies that
encouraged women to stay at home. The incentives included pensions (to which wives did not contribute) and tax credits so long as
their earnings were very low. At the same time, lack of child care,
elder care, and family leave made it very difficult for women to
reconcile work and family responsibilities. Women might work before marriage and even after, but once they had children they left
their jobs. The rising prosperity of this period made it possible for
families to survive on only one income. Given the huge cost of investment in lifetime workers, business did not want to invest in
women who might leave the workforce early in their lives; female
employees were placed on non-career tracks and served as buffers
who could be let go in times of economic downturn.[8] "The Japanese
system of convoy capitalism . . . was able to provide most citizens
with unprecedented economic security: care for those who needed
it, job security for workers, and a safety net that bought time for
firms to restructure their operations."[9] The fact that the private sec-

tor and women assumed many social welfare roles enabled the state to minimize social services and keep expenses low. In 1998, Patricia Boling wrote that clearly defined gender roles were thus the key to maintaining limited government involvement in welfare. "Indeed, enlisting and reinforcing informal values and practices, particularly gender roles and the behaviours they reinforce, is a pervasive strategy in Japan with regard to family policy—one which is easily overlooked because it looks like the absence of policy."[10] That remains largely true today, even though government policy has often appeared to favor modifications of gender roles.

This system, however, came under great stress as a result of globalization. There were strong pressures on Japan to open up its closed economic system, especially from the United States, which considered Japanese trade practices unfair. Japanese businesses chafed under the high costs inflicted by convoy capitalism, which made it harder to compete with the rising low-cost competitors like China. Women grew discontented with the demands of family life, pursued higher education, and sought careers, although employment opportunities were limited. The old system has dissolved but a new synthesis has not taken its place.

In a series of lucid articles, Retherford, Ogawa, and Matsukura explain the demographic causes of Japan's fertility decline. They attribute half of this decline in fertility to the rise in the mean age of marriage and to the increasing proportion of women who never marry.[11] The other half relates to low fertility of married couples. Japanese policy has proven ineffective at countering declining fertility. In the following pages, I first consider the causes for "late and less marriage," as Retherford, Ogawa, and Matsukura phrase it; then discuss low fertility within marriage; and finally, examine the failure of policy.

At the outset, it is important to point out something that is fairly obvious but rarely discussed: the impact of rapid social change on Japan. Rarely has any society—let alone a society usually described as "traditional" or "conservative"—changed so fast. On the national level, Japan went from feudalism to the first Asian industrial nation in a few generations, and from inward-looking to an ardent imperialist great power whose grand schemes of expansion ended in total defeat in World War II. Japan then repudiated militarism and transformed itself into the second largest economy in the world, a seemingly unstoppable juggernaut, only to get caught up in an extended period of stagnation, which was then compounded by global recession. The samurai as role model was replaced by the imperial warrior, who was in turn supplanted by the salary man. On the family level, the *ie* system was imposed as the legal model in the Meiji period only to be replaced relatively soon thereafter by the "modern" nuclear family whose survival itself was then called into question. The norm for marriage went from arranged to love matches in a generation or two after World War II. The Japanese were told during the war to have big families, after the war to have small families, and now Japan risks depopulation. The consequences of such rapid change are enormous yet hard to assess.

"Late Marriage and Less Marriage"?

Why is there an increasing number of Japanese women who never marry? An important reason for fewer marriages is the decline of arranged marriage without an adequate marriage market to replace it:

> The decline in arranged marriage appears to be closely linked to the end of universal marriage in Japan. . . . As late as 1960 the lifetime celibacy rate was only 2 percent for women and 1 percent for men. . . . The steep post–World War II decline in arranged marriage appears to be an important part of the explanation of why the lifetime celibacy rate started to rise gradually after 1960, and why it is expected to rise much more rapidly to very high levels in coming years.[12]

The change from arranged marriage to love marriage constitutes a fundamental shift in the nature of male-female relations. Arranged marriage meant the union of two houses in the interest of those houses. It also involved producing children as a matter of course to supply heirs and to perform religious duties to ancestors. Marriage and children were matters of duty, not choice. In a highly conformist society, 98 percent of women married and most had children. Japan went from arranged marriage to love marriage in record time, but that did not mean that social obligations thereby ceased. Far from it. Women still had obligations to their husband's aging parents (and often to their own as well). Moreover, the change to love marriage occurred without the development of the kinds of social skills that facilitate relations between the sexes. Western societies made the same transition, but over an extended time frame. Western literature indicates that at least since the seventeenth century, men and women sought to elude their parents' wishes and make love marriages. The problem in Japan may be more than the absence of a marriage market. For example, among young adults age eighteen to thirty-four years, "about 40 percent of females and about 50 percent of males said they had no friends of the opposite sex, let alone lovers or fiancé(e)s," a truly stunning figure.[13] In general, there seems to be a lack of easy friendships between the two sexes. Men and women tend to move in separate worlds, which makes it harder to find mates and engage in nongendered social relations. Coulmas argues that "if mutual love is a precondition of marriage, the possibility that no suitable partner will be found is implied." And the result is that unmarried life is becoming more common, and the stigma attached to it is declining.[14]

The problem of low birth rates is clearly a problem for the Japanese family. But that problem itself derives from the crisis faced by young men and women in Japan. Each sex is placed in an increasingly difficult position, which in turn makes their interrelationship problematic. It would seem that Japanese men and women do not reject the idea of marriage. They do not seek to live without marriage partners. Polls show that an overwhelming proportion of both sexes want to get married. Remaining single is not the result of conscious choice. Despite the wish to marry, increasing numbers of Japanese do not. The main problem seems to be discontent with the realities of marriage. "Given the highly inegalitarian nature of most Japanese marriages, the findings suggest that Japanese women are becoming increasingly dissatisfied with traditional marriage arrangements."[15] Men work long hours and either cannot or choose not to play much of a role in performing household chores or taking care of children. In addition, women do not want to live with or perhaps near a mother-in-law.

The expectations of Japanese women are high and often contradictory. Japanese women seem to want all the benefits of traditional marriage and fulfillment of the "three high desires"—"high educational background, high income, and high standing height."[16] At the same time, they want a husband willing to accept modern concepts of gender roles, which include playing a larger role in household chores. That is not astonishing, considering that the amount of time the average husband devotes to such chores each day is measured in minutes, not hours. Apparently, "between 1981 and 2001, the time that working married men spent on childcare and household chores has increased only modestly from 6 min[utes] to 34 min[utes] on weekdays and from 34 min[utes] to 1 h[our] and 4 min[utes] on Sundays."[17]

Well-educated, successful men in career tracks will probably lack the time (and perhaps the inclination) to share household responsibilities; men who out of choice (or more likely necessity) work part time or in temporary jobs may or may not be willing to accept modern gender roles but will lack the income necessary to support their wives. Perhaps at one time accepting "part-time" work was a way for a minority of nonconformist men to opt out of a rigid conformist culture, but now it is what many men are forced to do against their will. Women want to marry up in terms of education, but as the number of women with higher education rises, that prospect decreases, especially because men tend to prefer women with less education. Thus, highly educated women and poorly educated men have trouble finding spouses. There is a mismatch between the goals of the sexes. "The war of the sexes" seems to be a kind of cold war; it is frequently said that women are on a birth strike. If Chizuko Ueno is right, the reason for less marriage is the "unbridgeable gap between women's expectations for a 'partnership marriage' and men's desire for marriage with 'gender role assignments.'"[18]

Because marriage is no longer seen as a duty, women are willing to wait until they find the right man and remain single if they don't. The notion that a woman is like a Christmas cake that gets stale and can't be sold seems to be obsolete. Women seem willing to have no husband at all rather than the wrong husband. But because living on their own would lead to a decline of their standard of living, women tend to live with their parents. These young women have been given the pejorative epithet of "parasite singles." In 1998, 94 percent of nonstudent single women over 22 lived with their parents.[19] Some writers say that they contribute none of their salary to their parents and use their money for consumer goods. Others suggest that half of them do contribute money to the household. This discrepancy leads one to question how well the phenomenon is documented. Living with parents would presumably not facilitate entering into a love relationships and would tend to postpone marriage or make it less likely. It would decrease the likelihood of adjusting young people's standards of what constitutes an acceptable male. On the other hand, it is unlikely that most young working women could afford to live on their own, especially in places with high housing costs like Tokyo.

In some ways, young women living with their parents constitute a variant of the old stem family. In the stem family, the oldest son lives with his parents. The daughter-in-law serves the mother. Now it may be the actual daughter who remains and is served by the mother and supported by the father—but what happens later on, if the daughter never marries and the parents age? It can also be argued that in situations with only one female child in a family, that child may have to choose between a marriage in which she is expected to take care of her husband's family or not getting married so that she can take care of her own parents.

The labor market plays an important role in delaying marriage in two different ways. Women who manage to enter a career-track job may postpone marriage, knowing that marriage (and childbirth) will probably end any serious career. On the other hand, given the "diversification of the employment system," that is, the increase in part-time and temporary jobs, men may not feel that they can become heads of household. Thus, "the increasing trend of remaining single in Japan is due to the postponement of marriage both by those who still believe in the traditional gender norms as well as those who no longer believe in those norms."[20]

One factor that facilitates late or less marriage is that the sexual needs of both young men and women can be satisfied outside of wedlock. In the past men could frequent prostitutes, but women were more restricted. That is no longer the case. "The easy availability of pre-marital sex is another factor that has reduced the urgency of getting married and contributed to increases in the mean age of marriage."[21] Love hotels provide a safe and anonymous locale for sexual relations.

Inexplicably, however, young people's sexual needs seem to have declined as well, which may constitute an even more important reason for late or less marriage. There have been many previous studies concerning this subject, which might have been taken *cum granis salis.* Durex's Global Sexual Welfare Survey, conducted by Harris Interactive in 2006, found that only 34 percent of Japanese adults interviewed had sex weekly, and only 15 percent were satisfied. The respective percentages for the United States were 53 and 48; Singapore, 62 and 35; France, 70 and 25; and Italy, 76 and 36. Another writer declared in 2007 that Japanese people "in their 30s have sex only one-fifth as many times as, for example, the French."[22] It is harder to dismiss a recent study by the Japan Family Planning Association, an arm of the government, which indicated that 36 percent of males age sixteen to nineteen years had no interest in sex or even despised it, that 59 percent of female respondents said they were uninterested or averse to sex, and that 40.8 percent of married people said they had not had sex in the past month.[23]

Men's quandary is not much simpler than women's. Young men today are likely to have internalized the expectations of their fathers concerning normal standards of living and jobs. The stereotypical salary man gave himself up fully to his company but in exchange received lifetime job security, a good salary that enabled him to support his family, and access to generous retirement benefits. In this conformist society, status derived from a solid job. What then is the situation of young men who carry with them the expectations of a decent income and job security and end up in temporary or part-time jobs that often equate to full-time employment at part-time salaries with no security and few benefits? How can they marry and establish a family? How can they meet the expectations of young women who want husbands with higher or at least equal social status and income as their fathers? And how will they have learned the skills needed to share parenting responsibilities when their parents did no such thing? How do they maintain self-respect? Some attribute the low birth rate in Japan at least in part to the "enfeeblement of men" as a result of the destabilization of their social status.[24]

In her book *Lost in Transition*, Mary Brinton describes how the postwar social contract that guaranteed full-time jobs to both university and high school graduates in the 1980s broke down for high school graduates. Schools were no longer able to fulfill their old function of placing young people in jobs. Young people tended to blame themselves and lose self-confidence. One result (not the focus of her book) was later marriage and fewer children.[25] It has also been suggested that rather than risk rejection or summon the energy to maintain a modern relationship, many Japanese men simply "pay for affection in the country's ubiquitous hostess bars and brothels."[26]

One consideration not found in the literature on demography is the impact of gay rights. With the rise of gay rights, and even more of gay marriage in some countries, homosexuals are establishing their own separate communities. In the past, many gay men married and had families and either suppressed their sexual inclinations or practiced them in secret. That is less and less the case in the West today. Although Japanese gays do not have the same legal equality enjoyed in Northern Europe and some of the states in the United

States, such as the right to same-sex marriage, they may be less apt to marry and have children, thereby contributing to the falling birth rate. Nor can they adopt children, as is the case in some other countries.

One last factor making marriage more problematic for women is the rising tide of divorce. What happens to a woman who gives up her job and then finds herself divorced and without income (but suffering from the social stigma still attached to divorce)? Her husband may have a career-track job, but if she has abandoned a career to marry and have children, she will not be able to get it back. Prudence might dictate not getting married unless one is absolutely sure of the fiancé, and continuing to work and delaying children for at least a significant period of time. Both of these responses will drive down birth rates.

Decline of Fertility within Marriage

It is significant that in organizing a chapter on population issues in Japan, one can talk about "little and later marriage" and "fertility within marriage" without a discussion of fertility outside marriage. That would not be the case in the United States, where a significant number of births occur among young single women, often in their teens, or France and Sweden, where about half of all births occur to cohabiting couples, mostly in their late twenties and thirties. In Japan, few children are born out of wedlock, and cohabitation remains a rarity.

Cohabitation is not common in the developed states of Asia and Southern Europe. The case can be made that cohabitation could have beneficial results in Japan, helping to provide an alternative model of male-female relations with a greater place for spontaneity and shared roles. Perhaps in time this could help transform marriage as well. There is now widespread knowledge of nontraditional family behavior like child care, cohabitation, and nonmarital childbirth. It has been argued that the unattractiveness of the existing "marriage package" and greater awareness of nontraditional behavior may lead to changes in behavior as well.[27] Because "changes in values often occur in spurts in Japan," this change may occur quickly:

> Social disapproval of premarital sex was strong in Japan until the 1980s. When social disapproval is strong, latent receptivity to value change may grow for a while as a consequence of rising educational levels and other modernizing influences. At some point a new majority viewpoint emerges, and value change and behavioral change then diffuse rapidly through the population as the new values take hold and social disapproval of the previously proscribed behavior recedes. The time delay associated with the buildup of latent receptivity can be viewed as an aspect of cultural lag. This kind of rapid diffusion tends to be more visible in Japan than in many other countries because Japan is more highly integrated in the sense of shared values and good internal communication. This integration stems in large part from the high degree of homogeneity of Japan's population in such characteristics as language, ethnicity, and religion.[28]

One of the main reasons for low fertility in marriage is the difficulty of combining female employment and family. Even in the heyday of the male head of household system, employment of married women was common. But as we have seen, this employment was circumscribed. Women were not on a career track, but were temporary workers paid much less than men; in fact, they were paid less than in any other industrialized country.[29] They served as "shock absorbers" for the labor market, taken on in times of growth and laid off in times of recession.[30] There were strong incentives not to earn more than a limited amount:

> In 1998, the wife of a salaried employee who kept her earnings below ¥1.03 million ($8,583) avoided having to pay income tax, earned credit towards a basic pension without making her own contribution, qualified her husband for a dependent-spouse income tax break, and earned her family spousal bonuses and benefits such as subsidized housing.[31]

These benefits were lost once her salary crossed the maximum-amount threshold.

This helps explain why female employment followed an M-shaped curve. Women worked until they married (or had children), left employment to take care of their children, and then returned later on. Thereafter, they may have left the labor market to take care of aging parents or in-laws. Many Japanese women still operate within these norms, but a growing number of well-educated women who enter the labor force on a career track are reluctant to abandon it. The opportunity costs of having children are high for these women. The situation is complicated by the fact that many couples need two incomes. Now that male employment is more precarious, there is greater security if the woman also works. The decline in pensions and health-care benefits works in the same direction. Toro Suzuki suggests that the uncertainty created by Japan's poor economic performance—a problem that has persisted for decades—is "one of the major sources of lowest-low fertility in Japan."[32] Even for women who decide not to marry or not to have children, it is hard to achieve professional success in a labor market that discriminates against them. Although women make up almost half of Japan's workforce, they hold only 10.1 percent of managerial positions.[33]

Another reason for low fertility in marriage is the cost of children, especially the cost of formal education and cramming schools, or *juku*. Estimated cost of education through university ranges from $286,000 for the less expensive option to $630,100 for a more expensive option. In addition, one must add the costs of *jukus*, which may begin as early as elementary school.[34] These costs are no longer compensated by economic benefits. In an industrial or postindustrial world, not only will children not bring in family income, but they can no longer be counted on in the same way as a support in old age. At the same time, there is greater focus on self-realization and on consumer goods. Consequently, there is less interest in having children, especially on the part of those who themselves were only children.[35]

Patricia Boling talks about a "pervasive sense of crisis in Japan" over falling birth rates and an aging society:[36]

There is also evidence that child rearing has become a more onerous prospect. Many view contemporary urban Japan as a difficult environment in which to raise children. The poor infrastructure of public parks and green spaces means places to play freely and meet other children easily are limited, and many object to raising children while living in small, crowded apartments. . . . Secondly, as more women attempt to work throughout their adult lives, women increasingly experience stress over raising children single-handed. Because of the demands of their jobs, fathers are absent figures who do not help raise their children, which makes it especially difficult for women who continue to work while raising children, a trend which will worsen if the economy becomes more reliant on women's labour in the decades ahead. Thirdly, many dislike the burdens of raising children in a hyper-competitive environment, in which school entrance exams determine one's chances of success in life.[37]

Conversely, Toshihiko Hara writes that Japan has not yet developed a distinct "culture of childlessness" like Germany.[38] Women still claim that they want more than two children, whereas in Germany they want fewer than the replacement level of 2.1.[39]

The Failure of Policy

Although Japanese birth rates had been falling since World War II, the problem did not become widely known until the so-called 1.57 shock (the fact that the TFR fell to 1.57 in 1989). The birth rate had been very low in 1966, but that was taken as an anomaly because 1966 was considered to be an unlucky year to have children in the Chinese calendar. But there was nothing inauspicious about 1989, and since then birth rates have continued to fall. The problem has thus been clear to the government and general public for over two decades. Unlike Italy, Japan does not suffer from a lack of policy. On the contrary, there has been a series of policies, largely incremental in nature. Clearly, government action has not stemmed the tide of decline. The key question is why policy has been so ineffective.

At the outset, we must take note of an important factor that limits the role of government. Like Germany and Italy, the other members of the Axis, Japan's fascist-militarist wartime regime actively promoted pronatalism. The idea was to have enough Japanese to populate the new Japan. In the name of *umeyo fuyaseyo* (Have children! Boost the population!), the government pursued an aggressive pronatalist policy and attempted to restrict contraception. Then, after World War II, with the empire gone and millions of refugees repatriated to Japan, the birth rate seemed all too high. The government facilitated access to contraception and introduced the functional equivalent of abortion on demand. Japan became known as an "abortion paradise." When, after 1990, the government wanted to encourage fertility, the legacy of wartime policy meant that they could not explicitly advocate pronatalism. "The government's challenge . . . has therefore been to find ways of reversing the downward trend in fertility rates without using any of the aggressive tactics that worked (to some degree) in the 1940s and *without even openly discussing* the goal of influencing fertility rates."[40] The goal had to be making it possible for women to have the number of children they wanted, which is not very different from the policies followed successfully in Sweden and France, where emphasis today is rarely placed on the pronatalist dimension.

Japan has developed various programs to promote fertility, gender equality, and reconciliation of work and family. There is the equivalent of the French family allowance, but it is paltry and means, tested. Its value is about $42 for a child, rising to $84 for third children and beyond. Only about 20 percent of those eligible with children under three apply for it, possibly because the low benefits do not justify the administrative hassle involved in applying for it.[41] Japan provides no child allowance deductions for social security, no tax credits for income tax like the *quotient fiscal* in

France, and only some tax allowances, putting it near the bottom of these categories among countries that belong to the Organization for Economic Cooperation and Development.

Japanese women have long been entitled to eight weeks of paid maternity leave. In 1991, unpaid child care leave of up to ten months was authorized. As of 1995, 25 percent of salary would be paid for ten months. This was later raised to 40 percent in 2001. But because women faced discrimination on their return to work, only 64 percent of eligible females took maternity leave in 2002, and almost no men took paternity leave, which would have made them look ridiculous in the eyes of their bosses or fellow workers. Just as important, the legislation only covered full-time workers. But because the great majority of Japanese women workers are classified as part time (which, of course, does not mean they actually work part time), it is estimated that less than one-fifth of new mothers actually request and receive paid maternity leave.[42]

The government attempted to increase child care availability through successive Angel Plans and the Plus One program, but they have not eliminated waiting lists, especially in Tokyo. The government does not guarantee access. The big problem is providing long enough hours to meet the needs of couples who both work late. The problem with these programs remains the gap between the high declared goals and actual implementation. Although there has been progress in expanding child care, "eligibility for a childcare place is still fairly limited and usually based on the three-fold criteria of residence, both parents' full-time employment and the absence of relatives capable of delivering care."[43] It would seem that much child care is still provided by the family: the employment rate of mothers in three-generational households with the youngest child aged between birth and three is 41.4 percent, twice the proportion of women in two-generation households.[44]

Labor standards and employment practices comprise additional challenges. For example, the Equal Opportunities Employment Law of 1985, in the name of "equal treatment," ended prohibitions on night work for women and limits on overtime, which made it harder, not easier, to balance family and work.[45] Despite two decades of revisions in equal-opportunity legislation, the percentage of women in full-time regular jobs in the first decade of the twenty-first century has actually declined.[46]

At the root of this policy failure has been a high level of ambivalence between the desire to alleviate women's situation so that they can participate in the workforce and have more children and the obvious value of their continuing to shoulder the major responsibilities for child and elder care. These goals are largely contradictory, and so is government policy. As Boling points out, there is a contradiction between easing and exacerbating family burdens, the first reflected in formal policies and the second in informal practice. Formal policies represent *position taking*, but either because of lack of funding or their purely voluntary nature, businesses are "urged to" rather than "required to" comply, with results that are fairly predictable. In this realm at least, the government does not want to interfere with business because government policy is above all premised on economic success. But short-term economic interests are not the same as long-term interests, and support for business has not been translated into economic growth. At the same time, Japan has been reluctant to solve its problem of reconciling work and family through the kind of welfare state solutions practiced by Sweden. "Japan's political leaders are not interested in developing an interventionist, expensive welfare state along the lines of Sweden, which is often mentioned with a verbal crossing of the fingers as if to ward off evil."[47] Nor has there been much of an effort to reduce the long working hours that make family life nearly impossible. Yet today Sweden runs a low deficit, has a much lower national debt than Japan, and has recorded excellent economic growth. Rather than investing in imaginative programs to assist women (and ultimately, the entire society into the future), Japan has been bailing out failing banks, spending money on pork-barrel public works programs, and running huge annual deficits.[48]

Makoto Atoh and Mayuko Akachi have examined public spending in advanced industrial societies for programs supporting compatibility of work and family. Japan is at the bottom of the list for these kinds of program.[49] The enormous growth of an aging population also has an impact on family policy. To the extent that the government must choose between funding programs for seniors and children, it tends to opt for seniors. Pensions must be paid and the problem of incapacitated elderly people must be dealt with. Moreover, as we have noted earlier, there is nothing dramatic about declining birth rates and population decline. It is incremental; there is never an acute "crisis." It is the kind of problem that can be put off to another day. Children do not vote; seniors do, and parents of children are also children of aging parents. The ratio of support for the elderly versus for children is staggering in Japan. After the Fukushima disaster, the supposedly reformist Democratic Party of Japan government cut back plans to boost child care subsidies to support reconstruction, a decision that was backed by 83 percent of the population, according to a poll by Japan's largest newspaper.[50]

Decisionmaking in Japan on family and women's issues is a top-down process carried out by high-level bureaucrats. They are likely to have a broad policy perspective, but their perspective will tend to reflect their milieu and education. They are almost entirely male and unlikely to understand women's perspectives. The bureaucracy must take into account major interest groups in their policymaking; these interest groups are predominantly business related. Labor plays a relatively weak role overall, and even the unions represent the "haves" of the working class, which certainly do not include women. Women have little representation in Parliament, or among business elites or labor union leaders. Bureaucrats do not have to take into account women's interest groups militating for gender equality and work and family reconciliation because such groups barely exist. If government enacts gender equality policies, it is not as an end in itself but as a means to economic ends. The absence of women's voices is thus a major reason for the lack of a firm policy favoring social programs that would make possible family and work reconciliation based on women's perceived needs. Finnish scholar Tuukka Toivonen summarized the situation very well: "At this stage, it is possible to view the recent expansionary reforms as a largely *utilitarian project* by a predominantly male state machinery to rejuvenate Japan's birth rate and increase labour market participation, and to thereby sustain the social security system and economic growth."[51]

Leonard Schoppa attributes great significance to the fact that women have followed an exit strategy rather than a voice strategy. The effects of globalization and women's growing participation in higher education and the labor market might have led to a fundamental reshaping of the Japanese model. The point of Schoppa's book, however, is that fundamental change did not take place because the pressures for change were undercut by both business and women using limited exit strategies rather than working within the political system for change. Businesses chose to maintain the full-employment model for existing plants but increasingly selected locations abroad for new plants, leading to a hollowing out of the economy. Women chose *between* family and career. The result was a precipitous fall in the birth rate. Neither business leaders nor women battled for change in the political arena, leaving bureaucrats as the only advocates for change but rendering them ineffective. The result is that the Japanese model became less and less viable.

It would seem, however, that these two forms of exit are not parallel. Businesspeople achieve profitability through offshoring, although as Japan's big businesses become more multinational than Japanese, Japan as a nation is the loser. Women, however, do not achieve their goals by choosing *between* family and career. Nonetheless, Schoppa is right that women's passivity or political weakness is at the root of their failure to get what they want. In a society based on interest group politics, not having an interest group condemns you to defeat.

The failure to develop a national strategy is in the last analysis a reflection of the failure of the political system. After all, the bureaucracy is supposed to work for the government, not the other way around. But the Japanese political system has become increasingly dysfunctional. Plagued by factionalization, the long-serving Liberal Democratic Party proved unable to provide strong leadership. Although the Democratic Party of Japan seemed to be a fervent supporter of family-friendly policies when acting as the opposition party, it accomplished little in government.[52] Through five short-lived governments, its record in this area was nonexistent. Japan has become like the *bateau ivre* of Rimbaud. Even the Fukushima disaster, which some observers thought might provide the kind of challenge that would force the nation to rally around a new paradigm, has only divided and weakened government even further.

There seems to be a sense of defeatism in Japan today, which can be masked as stoicism. In 2010, after China had overtaken Japan as the world's second-largest economy, Norihiro Kato, an iconoclastic intellectual, published an op ed in the *New York Times* titled "Japan and the Ancient Art of Shrugging." He wrote,

> The rest of the world's population is still exploding, and we are coming to see the limits of our resources. The age of "right shoulder up" is over. Japan doesn't need to be No. 2 in the world, or No. 5 or 15. It's time to look to more important things, to think more about the environment and about people less lucky than ourselves. To learn about organic farming. Or not. Maybe you're busy enough just living your life. That, the new maturity says, is still cooler than right shoulder up.
>
> The new maturity may be the province of the young Japanese, but in a sense, it is a return to something much older than Mr. Ishihara and his cohort. Starting in the 19th century, with the reign of the Meiji Emperor, Japan expanded, territorially and economically. But before that, the country went through a 250-year period of comparative isolation and very limited economic growth. The experience of rapid growth was a new phenomenon. Japan remembers what it is like to be old, to be quiet, to turn inward.
>
> Freshly overtaken by China, Japan now seems to stand at the vanguard of a new downsizing movement, leading the way for countries bound sooner or later to follow in its wake. In a world

whose limits are increasingly apparent, Japan and its youths, old beyond their years, may well reveal what it is like to outgrow growth.[53]

Kato's article tries its best to make a virtue out of necessity. Willingness to accept economic decline and demographic decline is rebranded as evidence of maturity and wisdom. The problem is that if Japan's population continues to follow the downward trends of the past few decades, its unique way of life will not be reaffirmed. There will be no return to social stability. The demographic preconditions necessary for Japan's survival will be put at risk. Japan is on the threshold of entering into the low fertility trap. If policy tergiversations continue and if defeatism and denial prevail, Japanese society will become so firmly enmeshed in the trap that it may not be able to escape.

CHAPTER FIVE

Singapore: The Failure of Activism

The government has this thing called "Eat with Your Family Day,"
which I personally feel is ridiculous because you promote one
day in the entire year, out of 365 days, to eat with your family;
. . . then what happens to the rest of the time?

—SHIRLEY HSIAO-LI SUN, *Population Policy
and Reproduction in Singapore*

I N MANY RESPECTS, Singapore is a remarkable success. This small
city-state has become a transportation and financial hub for
Southeast Asia and one of the world's most prosperous nations. It
is also an extremely clean, safe, and orderly society with twenty-
first-century technology, which contrasts with its immediate neigh-
bors and compares favorably with the rest of the first world. Singapore's government has the ambitious goal of reaching a population
of 6.5 million. But fertility rates are very low, below a total fertility
rate (TFR) of 1.3; unless they rise, achieving growth or even pre-
venting decline will require levels of immigration that may be politically unsustainable. And population policy is a sensitive political
issue. Unhappiness about population policy led to two (relative)
electoral defeats for the ruling party, first in 1984 over the graduate
mothers' program and then again in 2011 over immigration policy.
So the government must tread carefully.[1]

The Productivist State

Since Singapore gained its independence in 1963, and since its sepa-
ration from federation with Malaysia in 1965, its independent development has been shaped by the hegemonic People's Action Party (PAP).
Singapore today, with all its virtues and limitations, is essentially

the creation of the PAP, although it was not created ex nihilo. Singapore under British rule was certainly a thriving colony. The regime has pursued a highly successful development strategy focused on economic growth, thereby reinforcing its legitimacy. Economics is the centerpiece of national strategy; consequently, the motivating force of population policy has been primarily economic.[2] As Shirley Sun argues, Singapore's goal is to create a productivist economy in which the hard-working are rewarded, as opposed to a social welfare state: "The central concern that has shaped the Singaporean government's policies in social provisions and population policies is molding "productive" citizens; the ideal citizen in the eyes of the state is an 'economically' productive one."[3]

Singapore is frequently referred to as a city-state. Although that is true, it is in many ways the opposite of the ancient Greek polis. Unlike the polis, Singapore is not self-sufficient—it does not have an agricultural hinterland surrounding an urban core. Its population does not trace itself to a common ancestor and worship common gods; religion and national identity are not fused. The ancient Greek polis did not extend citizenship to outsiders; Singapore actively seeks immigrants. Singapore has some of the characteristics of a nonstate actor, a vast corporation. But it would be wrong to deny the existence of Singapore nationalism.

Singapore today has state-of-the-art infrastructure, an advanced economy, sound finances, a good educational system, and a high standard of living. In principle, Singapore is a parliamentary republic with regularly scheduled elections. In practice, it is an authoritarian, one-party state. Singapore's government is technocratic and interventionist, but largely exempt from corruption. Since independence, it has been dominated by one exceptional leader, Lee Kuan Yew, who served as prime minister and then remained in the cabinet to mentor his successors. He is only now retiring from politics, at least in the sense of relinquishing any formal public position. Elections take place regularly, but the playing field is not level. Although alternation of power is almost unimaginable, opposition success in even a few districts is taken seriously and provokes serious reexamination of policy. In that sense, Singapore is a plebiscitary democracy, in which a party, rather than an individual, is the subject of periodic plebiscites.

The PAP can claim to have steered Singapore through extremely difficult times—overcoming the opposition of Communists in the trade unions, bringing Singapore out of a failed union with Malaysia, and ending communal violence. But, as Geraldine Heng and Janadas Devan point out, "by repeatedly focusing anxiety on the fragility of the new nation, its ostensible vulnerability to every kind of exigency, the state's originating agency is periodically reinforced and ratified, its access to wide-ranging instruments of power in the service of national protection continually consolidated."[4]

The key claim to the regime's legitimacy has been material success; under its leadership, Singapore has become a modern and very rich society. The PAP has demonstrated a high level of strategic thinking. Unlike many countries that opposed multinational investment, Singapore welcomed it. It succeeded through "firm central planning and strategic exploitation of global capitalism."[5] An export economy was built around heavy industry. The leadership recognized before the recession of the late 1970s that Singapore needed to go beyond manufacturing to a postindustrial economy based on services and successfully pursued that course. A two-track educational system was created with "hand and brain" streams.[6]

Building on the legacy of the British Singapore Improvement Trust efforts of the 1930s, massive public housing projects were erected, providing apartments for 80 percent of the population. This was not only to improve living conditions. Urban renewal eliminated the communist residential base in Chinatown as well as ethnic neighborhoods whose existence contributed to communal violence in the early 1960s. This communal violence deeply marked the PAP's leadership, who recognized these tensions as the country's Achilles heel. "The Singapore government has sought to create a synthetic amalgam in which the more traditional ethnic cultures are subordinated to a national ethos based on economic rationality and meritocracy. ... The Singapore government has 'strictly enforced racial harmony,' which seems to be a contradiction in itself."[7] Today, for example, residents in every public housing building must reflect the national ethnic ratio.

The population is defined by group rather than by individual identity. All citizens must be registered as belonging to an ethnic group—Chinese, Indian, Malay, or other. This means that their children study a second language defined by the government. For example, all Chinese must study Mandarin, even if their families spoke Cantonese or another dialect or were monolingual in English. The ethnic cultures that result are not so much the real cultural legacy of the family as an ersatz culture compatible with the interest of the State, which seeks above all to create racial harmony on its own terms.

Language played an important role in Singapore's self definition. The fact that English became one of the official languages—and the language of administration and instruction—facilitated Singapore's role in the global economy. It also eliminated the need to select a single official language from among the languages of the three ethnic groups, a choice that could only be divisive. Conversely, it allegedly opened the way to decadent Western values that the government tries to combat with "Asian values."[8] It has also been argued, however, that these "Asian values" are nothing more than Victorian values.[9]

The PAP combines laissez-faire and paternalist perspectives. Its ideology "comprises pragmatism, meritocracy, multiracialism, and, more recently and tentatively, Asian values or communitarianism."[10] Singapore is a combination of free market capitalism and a nanny state. It is not a welfare state. The state provides infrastructure, public order, and primary and secondary education (but there are fees for secondary education). The state does not offer the kind of basic services that most postindustrial societies (other than the United States) routinely provide, such as national health care, free college education, or retirement benefits. Singapore's mandatory savings fund, the Central Provident Fund, receives mandatory contributions from workers and employers (with some contributions from the government). It provides support for retirement, unemployment insurance, and medical care, as well as loans for down payments for housing, under terms set by the government. In turn, it is a major source of funding for public investment. Regarding retirement and elder care, the Confucian ideal that children are responsible for their parents' livelihood is enshrined in law. At the same time, the government feels that it has a right to tell people how to behave and to sanction misbehavior even on a micro level. A good example is the famous campaign against and ban of chewing gum in 1992. The publicity campaigns first to reduce birth rates and later to increase birth rates are not incongruous in Singapore, nor is the use of financial incentives and disincentives to affect behavior.

The Population Problem

Population policy today has two major goals: to increase birth rates, which are currently very low, and to encourage the right kind of immigration. Singapore's resident TFR sunk to 1.22 in 2009. There is, however, one fundamental policy precondition: it must preserve the existing ratio among Chinese, Indian, and Malay ethnic groups (approximately 75 percent Chinese, 14 percent Malay, and 9 percent Indian). That task is complicated by the differing birth rates of these groups. The Chinese (1.08) continued to have the lowest TFR, followed by the Indians (1.14) and Malays (1.82).[11]

Low birth rates in Singapore are the result of many of the same factors as in Japan, including less marriage, late marriage, and low fertility in marriage. As in Japan, fertility is almost entirely confined to marriage. In terms of less marriage, the number of people who remain single is relatively high, especially among Chinese women, and tends to increase with education. In 2010, 19 percent of all university-educated women were unmarried.[12] The causes for low marriage rates are similar to those in Japan. Gavin Jones enumerates several major reasons: "work pressures, housing affordability, and reluctance to live with (and later care for) parents-in-law."[13] Marriage is not required for sexual fulfillment; sex is available outside of marriage, as is contraception. Work culture gets in the way of social life. Avoiding marriage may even be a socially acceptable way of avoiding having children. Regarding declining marital fertility, the cost of education and housing, the problems of dual careers, and the fact that the burden of child raising falls mostly on women are adduced by Jones as relevant causal factors.

It was not always thus. Like Japan, in Singapore the demographic transition occurred later but faster than in Europe. In 1963, the TFR was 5.17; in 1972, it was 3.07; and in 1977, it was 1.82.[14] The result must have appeared paradoxical; within only a few years, a government that had vigorously advocated birth control was pursuing pronatalism with equal zeal. Surely this must have created some confusion on the part of the population. As Saw Swee Hock wrote: "Arguably, . . . Singapore could not have joined the ranks of new industrializing economies without limiting the growth of its population."[15] After World War II, Singapore's birth rate was extremely high. The TFR in 1947 was 6.55. The Family Planning Association, a private voluntary organization, received public funding from the new government of independent Singapore to provide assistance to individuals wanting to practice contraception. Indeed, the birth rate had declined to 4.95 in 1964. But the Singapore government clearly did not put its faith in the continuation of this trend. Just six weeks after Singapore's August 9, 1965, withdrawal from federation with Malaysia, the government issued a white paper on family planning. On January 7, 1966, an Act of Parliament was passed without debate creating the Singapore Family Planning and Population Board. Subsequently, the government initiated a series of programs, including postpartum distribution of contraceptives and legalization of abortion in 1969 with some restrictions, followed by abortion on demand in 1974. Abortion became a common practice. In 1975, there were 321 abortions per 1,000 live births, going up to 477.3 in 1977.[16] In 1969, during the debate on the abortion bill, Lee Kuan Yew declared: "The quality of the population would deteriorate . . . if the present trend of less educated parents . . . producing larger families than better educated . . . parents continued. We will regret the time lost if we do not take the first tentative step toward correcting a trend which can leave our society with a large number of the physically, intellectually, and culturally anemic."[17] Eugenics was thus a declared goal of government policy from early on. Voluntary sterilization enacted in 1969 liberalized sterilization to virtually sterilization on demand in 1974. As of 1977, 60,689 women were sterilized in a population of 2,325,300. In support of these programs, the government instituted a series of incentives and disincentives, some of which involved reversing existing policies that favored large families.

By the 1980s, Singapore was pursuing its new orientation toward the creation of an economy based on services and knowledge. The decline of birth rates in the 1970s and 1980s was exceeded by the decline in the birth rates of well-educated women. This troubled Lee Kuan Yew, who, as his previous statement made clear, was a believer in eugenics, even though elsewhere it was widely discredited as a "science" after the experiences of World War II. He concluded that intelligence was 80 percent determined by genes; therefore, the unfavorable ratio between the birth rate of educated and uneducated women posed a threat to the future of the nation. Lee Kuan Yew's personal convictions quickly became state policy. The result was a period of population policy based explicitly on eugenic concepts, as interpreted by the prime minister—and the famous (or notorious) graduate mother program. The problem is that if genes determine success, then the existing class structure approximates biological reality. If intelligence is transmissible, the social structure will be replicated in the next generation. The goal then would be to maximize each individual's full development within an essentially caste system. As Vivienne Wee argued, there are important consequences for education: a "rigid hierarchization of children, with their different 'inherent characteristics.'"[18] Wee cited Lee Kuan Yew as stating that there is approximately one natural leader in a thousand. She argues that "the entire educational system in Singapore may be understood as a nationwide searching and testing device for innate leadership."[19] An educational system based on tracking at an early age is likely to replicate and perpetuate class differences.

The eugenics program was previewed in the prime minister's National Day speech of August 14, 1983. The speech began by praising Singapore's economic performance during the previous year and raising the rhetorical question of how this success was achieved. Lee summarized Singapore's struggles to achieve "stability, discipline, efficiency, and security." The effort to achieve maximum potential requires development of "inherent capabilities." The prime minister then introduced the idea that 80 percent of intelligence derives from genes; unfortunately, however, better-educated women in Singapore then and now have fewer children:

> Our economy will falter, the administration will suffer, and the society will decline. For how can we avoid lowering performance when for every two graduates [with some exaggeration to make the point], in 25 years time there will be one graduate, and for every two uneducated workers there will be three? Worse, the coming society of computers and robotics needs more, not less, well-educated workers.

Lee seems to have believed that because the entire population received compulsory education and there were no remaining rural pockets of able but uneducated persons, higher education and economic success reflected inherent and transmittable genetic superiority. It has been argued that there was also a racial element in the equation: graduate mothers were mostly Chinese, and less-educated women with higher birth rates were Malay and Indian.[20]

Lee's speech was followed by measures to increase the birth rate among graduate women, including state-sponsored matchmaking by a newly formed Social Development Unit, income tax benefits, and, most controversially, priority for primary school registration (which was soon repealed). At the same time, a $10,000 bonus was instituted to encourage low-income women to undergo sterilization. Hospital fees for childbirth were also raised for lower-class women to discourage pregnancy. This policy was extremely unpopular and led to some unaccustomed opposition success in parliamentary elections. The result was that eugenics became an implicit rather than an explicit element of policy. But it has never disappeared as a significant element of policy and, as discussed here, is one reason that pronatalism has not succeeded in Singapore.

With the continued plunge in the birth rate to well below replacement levels, government concern grew. This concern was conveyed in an August 4, 1986, speech by Goh Chok Tong, first deputy prime minister and later prime minister, titled "Singapore's Long March." Singapore's struggle for survival and development was as difficult as Mao's Long March, and by extension Singapore's future remained precarious. In escaping from the recession, Singapore faced the physical constraints of being a small country with few resources, as well as demographic constraints. At a time of aging populations, Singapore was not producing enough babies to maintain a stable population, threatening the nation's prosperity and even its security. Goh also spoke about the importance of national harmony and referred to Sri Lanka, which was just beginning a civil war that was to last twenty-five years, as an example of how ethnic tension can threaten a nation's future. This may have been an oblique reference to differential birth rates among ethnic groups in Singapore, requiring Chinese immigration in order to maintain the traditional ratio (to be discussed later).

Shortly thereafter, the government adopted a new slogan of "Have Three or More If You Can Afford It" and began to modify antinatalist policies and develop pronatalist policies. But there was great reluctance to eliminate all antinatalist policies for fear that this "might lead to excessive births among certain segments of the population, such as the poor and lesser-educated groups."[21] These restrictions were further modified in the second round of reforms in 2004. Mirroring the gravity of the situation, policies became more generous and less restrictive.

The importance of this subject to the Singapore government was made clear by the fact that Prime Minister Lee Hsien devoted part of his 2004 National Day speech to the joys of babies and children before outlining a series of measures designed to help reconcile work and family life. (The speech was followed by a propaganda campaign along the same lines.) These measures included priority for families with children in access to public housing and to down payments on housing; extension of paid maternity leave to twelve weeks; income tax deductions and special tax rebates for children; institution of a five-day work week and of marriage and paternity leave (three days); two-day child care leave; flex time for female civil servants; a baby bonus; outright yearly grants during a child's first six years, as well as matching grants; child care subsidies; and tax breaks for maids and grandparents engaged in child care.

The nature of these policies says a great deal about the ruling party's philosophy and the instruments it chose to wield. First, the PAP perceives the citizen as a *homo economicus*. The idea is that financial benefits will modify behavior: "The government's new policies are targeted at reducing the narrow economic costs of child-bearing. Such costs are only one among many factors influencing rational fertility decisions and other influences are working in the opposite directions to increase perceived costs."[22]

Second, the benefits are monetary because, in general, the government provides few services. For example, the government gives tax breaks and subsidies for child care and participates in building child care facilities but does not provide child care itself.[23]

Third, the benefits are generally universal rather than means tested, but with an important qualification. In the social welfare policies of many countries, there is a trade-off between universal policies and policies that are means tested. The reason is that with limited funds, governments may want to focus on the most disadvantaged. In Singapore, however, for eugenic purposes, the government has wanted to encourage educated women to have children and discourage poorer and less-educated women from having many children. Policies have thus aimed at favoring the well-off rather than the poor. Because some benefits only apply to those with higher incomes, in some ways there is a kind of reverse means testing that excludes the poor.

Fourth, the government appeals to nationalist feelings and concerns about the future of the country. Nationalism, however, may not be intense in a country that is often portrayed as Singapore Inc.; moreover, this kind of exhortation has never had much appeal anywhere.

The most significant policy was the institution of flex time for mothers in the civil service, but it was not extended to the private sector.

These policies failed to increase birth rates. According to official statistics, total births and resident births continued to decline in 2008 and 2009.[24] In 2008, the TFR was 1.28, but it fell to 1.22 in 2009. The TFR for all ethnic groups in 2009 was below replacement. The TFR gap between university-educated women and those with less than a secondary-level education narrowed, only because the number of children born to the latter fell even faster than that of children born to the former. The number of unmarried women, age of marriage, and mother's age at the birth of the first child have continued to increase.

Why have these policies failed? The Singapore government treats its citizens as *homini economici*, and they respond as such. The benefits provided do not come near the cost of providing for a child. Subsidies for child care or tax breaks for parents who hire nannies will be welcome—but they will not convince the reluctant to become parents and may not suffice to persuade the undecided. The amount of child care leave, for example, is paltry. As Gunnar Myrdal pointed out, having children induces poverty. Unless the society assumes a large part of the cost, average people will not be able to afford them. Using a basic economic calculus, most Singaporeans conclude that government benefits are not sufficient to make children affordable.

The government has helped to create a consumerist mentality, but there probably is no mentality less compatible with having children. The Singapore government has based its raison d'être on prosperity and has helped make Singapore a consumer society par excellence. Most public places in Singapore are shopping malls. Having children does not fit comfortably into a consumerist mentality or, for that matter, with Singapore's typically long working days. Nor are children compatible with the rhythms of life of many young people who commute from the periphery of the island to work downtown. The normal day for a couple involves commuting, meeting friends afterward at a food court, and maybe returning home late at night. This pattern would have to be completely rethought if and when a couple decides to raise children.

There are many photos in Singapore of the old, squalid housing lacking running water and basic sanitary conditions. Eliminating the *kampung* and creating modern high-rise apartments is one of the PAP government's claims to legitimacy. The older public housing resembles low-income public housing projects in the United States; the newer ones are much nicer, but they are much higher (i.e., very-high-rise apartment buildings). Public housing has disrupted the old extended families, although there are now policies facilitating a regrouping of parents and children in the same neighborhood, in part so that grandparents can care for the children of working women. Each public housing complex boasts a small children's playground, but it does not really look like a place where children would like to play. Finally, there is something anomalous about a severe, paternalist state instructing young people that they should date, have fun, marry, and procreate. In a society where open dissent is dangerous, a birth strike may be a particularly effective form of revolt.

In a series of articles based on interviews and focus groups, Shirley Hsiao-Li Sun documents the response of Singapore citizens to the government's pronatalist policies. These responses help explain why government policies do not bring about desired results.

Women complain that policies providing for maternity and child care leave are incompatible with the realities of how business really works. With the exception of civil servants, women who wish to combine career and family are hindered by the fact that both maternity leave and paid child care leave are partially paid for by employers who are reluctant for employees to take leave. Employees fear being fired if they request leave, despite the law. Job insecurity is thus a major barrier to reconciliation of work and family. The solution offered by some of the women interviewed was that these programs should be paid for by the government. They also suggested creation of a flex-time system in the private sector; currently flexible hours exist only for civil servants. One woman ridiculed a favorite piece of government propaganda:

> The government has this thing called "Eat with your Family Day," which I personally feel is so ridiculous because you promote that one day in the entire year, out of 365 days, to eat with your family. . . . Then what happens to the rest of the time?[25]

Men interviewed indicated that they did not believe paid paternity leave was an important factor in deciding whether to have children. In any case, they were unlikely to request it. The work culture of Singapore is incompatible with making use of paternity leave. Only if paternity leave were mandated and financed by the government, like the National Service, would they be likely to take it. (Reservists are paid by the government when called to duty.) What concerned men most of all was their ability to serve as breadwinners, still considered a male role, but not easy to fulfill. Men feel insecure about their jobs, especially lower-level workers, who are threatened by competition from the large number of immigrants in the country. "The state needs to reconsider the economic production-at-all-cost approach and become more proactive in supporting workers' right to paid employment *and* family life."[26] Then again, Singapore is dominated by a work culture. Fathers are use to utilize parental leave. As one male informant said: "You're in Singapore. In Singapore, you need to work, you don't work you die. . . . Even if the government gives support, cool. What about the private sector? How are they going to react to it?"[27]

Because Singaporeans are part of a globalized economy, they are globally aware and compare Singapore's population policies unfavorably to those of other countries:

> In sum, first, while the Singaporean government has legitimized the implementation of "work/family balance" policies by pointing to the existence of such policies in European countries, the citizens interviewed for this study questioned the effectiveness of such policies by invoking their knowledge of practices such as flexible workplace provisions in England and Germany and shorter work hours in Australia. They also emphasized the *comparatively* unsympathetic nature of Singaporean employers. Second, while the government resists the idea of more generous and universal state-provided subsidies, the citizens elaborated on their perceptions of such benefits in Australia, Brunei, Canada, France, and the U.K. Respondents suggested that more direct state financial subsidies, especially subsidies for education and young children's daily needs, would encourage and further strengthen a sense of national belonging. Third, the citizens invoked the notion of migration to signal their discontent with current state policy provisions.[28]

Sun concludes that "when the perspectives of citizens are constantly ignored by the state, migration, a form of moral protest, becomes an option to be taken seriously."[29]

Singaporeans complain that government policies do not benefit the average citizen, that government programs such as the baby bonus are insufficient.[30] Many people cannot afford to take advantage of the matching funds provided by the Children Development Co-Savings account. In addition, most citizens are unaware of the details of government programs. Most important, the major form of support for families with children is tax rebates, but "70 per cent of the resident population has an average monthly per capita household income of only $1,580, which means no tax and therefore no tax rebates."[31] As one interviewee said, "Honestly speaking, they have not deducted a cent of tax for my employment of more than ten years, because there is nothing for them to deduct."[32] Thus, income tax deductions only benefit the upper middle class and the wealthy. Sun concludes that Singapore practices a de facto "differential class-specific pronatalism."[33]

Another criticism of government policy is the contradiction between the government's emphasis on "Asian values"—which presumably imply the male-dominated "traditional family" with the husband as breadwinner—and its support for equality in higher education and female participation in the workforce. These "Asian values" include filial piety—care for parents comes first and then for children. Many women opt out of having children, knowing that they must care for parents later in life. The fact that the government provides monetary support to families with children, as opposed to social services to help women reconcile work and family, reinforces the traditional family. As Peter McDonald writes: "Thus, expenditure on tax transfers is consistent with the male breadwinner model of the family while expenditures on services is consistent with a gender equity model."[34] The problem is that in advanced industrial societies, the traditional family equates to lower rather than higher birth rates. Women are objects of policymaking, not subjects, in part because of the absence of a women's movement in Singapore.[35] Consequently, women are placed in an impossible situation:

> While the state's intent was to lure mothers back into the workforce to ensure that its manpower needs were met, the message sent to both men and women was very clear: childcare is the sole responsibility of the mother. . . . When women weigh the pros and cons of family formation, many often end up overwhelmed by the perceived costs of retreating from their careers and the direct costs of child-rearing.[36]

Without greater gender equality, it will be impossible to raise the birth rate.

The Immigration Alternative

The government of Singapore must certainly be aware that its pronatalist policies have failed. As Professor Saw Swee-Hock wrote in 2007, "The recent recognition that despite the introduction of a comprehensive postnatalist programme, fertility will never return to replacement level to sustain . . . the population size in the future, has resulted in a big shift in the national population programme towards immigration as the key answer to replenish the population in the years ahead."[37] As Lee Kuan Yew declared in 2012, "Like it or not, unless we have more babies, we need to accept immigrants."[38] The Singapore government is on record stating that it wishes to increase population to 6.5 million. Given Singapore's lowest-low birth rates, the only solution is massive immigration.[39] Presumably, immigration is also consistent with eugenics considerations: attracting educated, successful immigrants will bring in the right kind of people into Singapore. But such a policy is not without perils.

Increasing immigration has been a hallmark of Singapore policy for the last decade. Under British colonial rule, much of Singapore's population was born elsewhere. In 1947, 39.3 percent of the population was not born in Singapore or Malaysia; in 1957, 27 percent. In 1970, as Singapore began to forge its own national identity, only 2.9 percent of the population was from abroad. But the proportion has risen rapidly: 10.3 percent in 1990, 18.7 percent in 2000, and 25.7 percent in 2010.[40]

The growth rate of permanent residents in Singapore over the last two decades has risen dramatically; the annual growth of permanent residents since 2004 was never lower than 6.5 percent and attained 11.5 percent in 2009. The growth of nonresidents was also very high, including a peak of 19 percent in 2008. In 1990, the citizen population of Singapore constituted 2,623,700 out of a total population of 3,047,100; in 2010, only 3,230,700 out of 5,076,000 were citizens.[41] Liu Hong points out that high school students from China receive full scholarships to junior colleges and colleges in Singapore if they agree to work at least six years upon graduation.

Singapore draws on two kinds of immigrants: professionals who can become permanent residents and citizens, and others who come for short-term contracts and are segregated from the rest of the population. But there are also high-skilled workers, many of them from China, who obtain employment passes, not work permits, and who may have access to permanent residency status.[42] That means that immigrants introduce a perceived threat to the economic well-being of Singapore citizens on many levels of the economy—and this threat leads to resentment.

Because of its high wages and standard of living, Singapore can draw on the large Chinese diaspora and citizens of China. Presumably, this requires less effort at acculturation and integration than in many other countries that draw on ethnically and culturally different populations. Nonetheless, it is not all that simple to transform a citizen of China, for example, into a typical Singaporean. In 2008, the number of new permanent residents in Singapore was 79,167, and in 2009, 59,460. The total number of citizen births in 2009 was 31,842. That is to say that there were about twice as many new permanent residents as citizen births.

Immigration became a hot button issue in the May 2011 elections, in which the opposition won an unprecedented 40 percent of the popular vote (although only six seats out of eighty-one, because the electoral system is constructed to make it difficult for the opposition to get into Parliament). This was an electoral tsunami. The *Economist* wrote:

> The opposition tapped a vein of resentment towards the PAP. Despite its success in making Singapore a rich, clean, law-abiding, and pleasant city, the PAP has alienated many voters. A common perception is that it has lost touch with the concerns of the less well-off—about rising prices, especially of housing, and about the rapid influx of immigrants, notably from China. Of the population of just over 5 [million], about a quarter are immigrants.[43]

But looking at Internet Web sites (e.g., *Temasek Review Emeritus,* which presumably evades the government's famous libel laws muzzling the press) gives a sense of the raw anger some feel about government policy. For example, one response:

> Folks, if PAP wins a majority for another 5 years, they will bring in more foreigners to take away our jobs, convert PRs to New Citizens. New Citizens will Vote for PAP as they like PAP liberal foreigner policy and hope to bring their entire families to Singapore at the expense of Natives. It will also be out of gratitude that New Citizens Vote for PAP.
>
> When Natives become the minority say 25 percent of 6.5 million, PAP will say PRs/Foreigners are 75 percent of 6.5 million and they take up majority of our jobs, we need them and cannot kick them out. All Natives will have to LIVE as minority and being marginalized forever.[44]

The same is true for readers' comments in the *Online Citizen*. The latter's editorial of April 26, 2012, presents a reasoned argument for why Singaporeans do not have children and why immigration does not solve the problem:

> For starters, what sane parent-to-be wants to bring up a child who is going to have to face the rigors of one of the most competitive and stressful education systems in the world, the scholastic equivalent of the Hunger Games?
>
> Who, stuck on the treadmill of economic survival, has time to take a breather to nurture the romances that form the building blocks of stable family units?
>
> And perhaps it is here that the recent debate on income inequality becomes relevant: If you belong to a low-income group in Singapore, how are you going to afford to have children? Would you want to run the risk of your children falling into the same wage rut as you? . . .
>
> If native Singaporeans feel increasingly disinclined to have babies, and the government's only solution is to replace Singaporeans by evermore desperately giving out citizenship to foreigners, this all looks a bit like a race to the bottom.

These comments tend to echo the focus groups cited in Shirley Sun's book. The degree of bitterness at immigrants is reflected in the fact that 77 percent of respondents in a poll said they were not proud of an immigrant from China who received the first individual Olympic medal for Singapore in fifty-two years![45] The question that arises, therefore, is whether the government will have to rethink the premises of its failed pronatalist program, which in turn might force it to reconsider its refusal to provide social services for parents rather than just financial incentives.

There may be no choice. Recent projections show that with current TFR and no immigration, the population of Singapore would peak at 3.68 million in 2020 and decline to 3.03 million in 2050. With immigration of 30,000 a year, population would peak at 4.89 million in 2050; immigration of 60,000 would allow Singapore to reach 6.76 million in 2050. An increase in the TFR to 1.85 with no immigration would lead to a peak of 3.73 million, followed by decline.[46]

There was some reason to think that the political leadership was examining options. A recent article by Tommy Koh, former long-time ambassador to the United States and rector of Tembusu College of the National University of Singapore, titled "What Singapore Can Learn from Europe," indicated that the political elite was at least considering a new approach to population policy and social policy as well. Koh compared Nordic social policies favorably with Singapore. He stressed that the Gini index was much more favorable in the Nordic states than in Singapore and suggested that Singapore should "reduce the supply of cheap foreign workers or introduce a minimum wage to target specific industries." He contrasted the low birth rate in Singapore with the relatively high birth rates in Nordic states, which he believed were caused by four factors: "the availability of convenient, affordable, and good childcare; good work/life balance; an excellent and relatively stress-free education system; and the relative absence of male chauvinism."[47] It was easy to imagine that this article could have been a trial balloon for a reorientation of Singapore policy in the direction of becoming more of a welfare state, in which increased birth rates would eventually eliminate the need for high levels of immigration. Another, more academic analysis, "Inequality and the Need for a New Social Compact," discussed the increase of inequality in Singapore and its negative consequences. It critiqued "market fundamentalism" and emphasized the need to question long-standing assumptions, such as "the idea that sturdier safety nets will erode economic incentives and undermine competitiveness."[48] It advocated a "new social compact founded on the ideas of an activist, more redistributive state, one that aims to strike a better balance between social protection and individual responsibility."[49] Public spending could be increased from a very low 16 percent of gross domestic product to about 25 percent in a ten- to twenty-year time frame.[50] Such a change in policy might also have the potential to increase the birth rate, although population issues are not explicitly discussed in the report. The nature of Singapore's political system makes it possible to imagine significant and rapid policy changes that could have an important and beneficial impact on population. It was not clear, however, whether such changes were compatible with the productivist state. Subsequent policy statements made it apparent that the government was not about to change course.

Conclusion: Can Government Policy Reverse Declining Birth Rates?

B IRTH RATES ARE DECLINING in almost all developed and many developing societies. The examples of France and Sweden show that well-designed family policies can mitigate this trend. France and Sweden succeeded by devoting significant financial resources to family policy and supporting women's need to reconcile work and children. The success of a similar approach in other countries depends on two main factors: first, whether adequate national resources can be allocated, despite the decline of the welfare state; and second, whether the implications of gender equality will be accepted by political leaders and the population.

Birth rates have fallen in almost all developed countries and in many developing societies as well. The role of the family as an economic unit has declined, as children have lost their economic value and become an economic liability, whose cost is often prohibitive. Contraception, especially the pill, has made it possible to separate sex and procreation and drastically reduce the number of "unplanned" pregnancies. With remarkable speed, the role of women has changed; women in the workforce are now the norm, and full-time homemakers are becoming rare. The "traditional family," that is, the family that emerged in the postwar era, is being transformed. *Without government intervention, birth rates tend to fall below replacement level in advanced industrial societies.*

This brings us back to the key question of this book. Can governments reverse or mitigate declining birth rates? The chapters on Sweden and France make it clear that public policy has been effective in raising birth rates in these countries. But Sweden and France developed their policies half a century ago. Are the Swedish and French examples still relevant? Can government policy reverse falling birth rates in other countries today, under the new conditions of the twenty-first century?

The Swedish Social Democrats came to power at the height of the Great Depression. They understood how the failure of government action in Germany to combat the Great Depression brought Hitler to power. By extension, resolving the economic crisis in Sweden was a matter of life or death for Swedish democracy. It was fortunate that one of the intellectual heavyweights of the Swedish left was Gunnar Myrdal. Myrdal, whose economic ideas were akin to those of Keynes, helped formulate the Social Democrats' activist approach to the Depression. Together with his wife, Alva, Myrdal had also written a best seller on the population crisis in 1934. Their influence was instrumental in creating a new holistic social model that addressed the economic and demographic crises in an integrated way.

A similar thing happened in post–World War II France. The defeat of 1940 induced deep reflection on the part of resistance leaders about the long-term roots of France's decline.[1] Their analysis centered on the stagnation of France's demographic, economic, and social development, which was widely described as "Malthusian." If France was to regain the status to which de Gaulle and other French leaders aspired, a new dynamism was needed. Population growth was an indispensable element of that synergy, which also included economic growth, social justice, and national security. France would *plan* itself out of industrial underdevelopment and demographic stagnation. Both the Swedes and French based their policies on an activist state that engaged in economic planning as well as redistribution.

Before the 1930s, in the days of the liberal state when limited government and low taxes prevailed, the only methods available to encourage higher birth rates were hortatory or punitive. Hortatory approaches urging women to make babies for the fatherland (or motherland) were ineffective. And punitive approaches were incompatible with political democracy. The welfare state, conversely, could provide money or services to *encourage* behavior deemed to be in the national interest or, even better, provide the means for people to do what they really wanted to do but could not otherwise afford. If women really wanted more children but could not afford them, the state could help them out. State policy could narrow the gap between the number of children that women said they wanted and the number of children they were actually having. *Indeed, that is the basis of all modern pronatalist policy—the belief that appropriate public policy can narrow that gap.*

The Depression demonstrated the inability of classical liberal capitalism to be self-regulating. An interventionist state was necessary to engage in countercyclical policies.[2] The social consequences of the Great Depression—the polarization of society, the emergence of fascism and Nazism, the spread of communism, and the resulting march to war—made clear the need for extraordinary action by government to guarantee the social security of the population. Invisible hands did not work or they worked too slowly, leaving unbearable social destruction in their wake. By analogy, one could argue that *demography was no more self-regulating than the economy.* The precepts of modern social science would guide government in solving demographic problems just as the principles of modern economics would guide governments in maintaining prosperity. This period constitutes a kind of Keynesian moment in European and American history.

Swedish and French demographic policies reflected this understanding. What is striking is the prescience of the ideas that the Myrdals proposed in the 1930s (discussed in chapter 1):

- Pronatalist policy makes possible a synthesis of leftist and conservative ideals.

- Contraception is a precondition for a modern pronatalist policy.

- The success of any pronatalist policy requires acceptance that ways must be found "to allow married women both to work and have a career and at the same time to have children."

- Children are an economic burden for their family. The precondition of higher birth rates is such that "a large part of the economic burden of bringing up children must be passed from the individual family to society as a whole." Redistribution of wealth must take place not only between rich and poor but also between those with few or no children and those with many.
- Successful population policy involves eliminating the obstacles that prevent ordinary people from following their wishes to marry and have children.
- The quality of population is just as important or even more important than the quantity. This involves providing children with better housing, nutrition, health care, and education.
- Programs must be universal rather than means tested, providing services rather than cash grants.

With the exception of the last, these principles are common to both Swedish and French policies and to most countries pursuing successful population policies.

Sweden and France implemented policies that were consistent with Myrdal's ideas. The result was the creation of a virtuous circle. Birth rates approached replacement level, as women having two children became the norm. The need for explicit pronatalist policy goals receded and the focus shifted to satisfying the needs of women, children, and the family. Population stability was largely achieved. Even though the population continued to age, an acceptable dependency ratio (the percentage of working-age adults compared with nonactive citizens) was sustained. This in turn maintained the state's financial stability. The welfare state financed pronatalist policies; reasonably high birth rates in turn stabilized the welfare state. A new demographic equilibrium was attained.

What remains to be seen is whether nations achieving this kind of sustainable demographic situation will be the exception or the rule. At present among advanced postindustrial nations, birth rates of near replacement or moderately low levels exist in the northern areas of Western Europe (other than German-speaking lands), the British Isles, and France, but nowhere else in Europe. The birth rate is extremely low in all developed nations in Asia. The United States has maintained a replacement-level birth rate despite very limited support for families with children, a remarkable case of American exceptionalism. In short, very low birth rates are the rule, not the exception.

What has prevented other developed countries from pursuing the policies that France and Sweden have successfully followed? Our other case studies provide the basis for answers.

A key factor in failing to develop pronatalist programs is *timing*. The golden age of the welfare state, a period of exceptional economic prosperity in the developed world, occurred between the end of World War II and the 1970s. Following that period, the welfare state was assailed by neoliberalism and undermined by economic and financial crises. In countries where the modern welfare state did *not* fully emerge, no effective state policy directed at countering low birth rates was likely to develop. If the problem of low birth rates emerged *after* the decline of the welfare state, it was also unlikely that major (and costly) programs directed at population problems would be implemented.

Other factors that work against the development of pronatalist policies are *values and ideology*: the political influence of religious organizations, especially but not exclusively the Catholic Church, that defend the "traditional family" and oppose public social services that support working mothers; strong familialist values and opposition to gender equality in the home but also in the workplace; the legacy of fascism and communism, which discredited the concept of pronatalism in nations where they ruled; ideological commitment to a rigid vision of free market capitalism, rendering the idea of public social services unacceptable; and consumerist values that make children a potential inconvenience.

Additional factors are *politics and economics*: an ineffective state or stalemated political system, thanks to which family policy cannot be enacted and implemented; acute and chronic fiscal problems that preclude new and expensive social programs; and, on the part of individual young people, precarious employment and fear of downward mobility.

Most of these factors explain the Italian dilemma. Italy is not a case of the failure of policy but of the failure to develop policy. The Italian birth rate did not fall below replacement until the 1970s; recognition of a serious and chronic problem only came much later, when the underdeveloped Italian welfare state was already shaky. With the exception of a rigid commitment to the free market, all the above factors impeding the development of modern pronatalist policies apply to Italy: opposition by the powerful Catholic Church; strong familialist values; the legacy of fascism (used more as an alibi than as a real cause, one suspects); consumerist values (which don't prevent people from having children in Italy but limit families to one or two); an ineffective state and stalemated political system; chronic financial problems, currently epitomized by Italy's involvement in the euro crisis; and the difficulties that young people encounter in finding decent employment. As discussed above, the causes of Italy's demographic problem are overdetermined; there is no mystery why Italy does not have an effective policy. Nor have other nations in Southern Europe fared much better.

Italy's population problem is somewhat mitigated by high levels of immigration. Yet opposition to immigration constitutes the major program of one of the former governing parties, the Northern League. A cynic might conclude that this was not pure coincidence. The Berlusconi government encouraged importation of cheap labor, satisfying many of the prime minister's business supporters while at the same time providing grist for the mill of the Northern League.

It might be argued that only an acute and systemic crisis in Italy will lead to the kind of thoroughgoing reform that can turn the country's economy around and make possible a real population policy as well. That at least would be compatible with the old idea that history is made by challenge and response. But there is no guarantee that a crisis will produce needed reform. The word "crisis" has long been trivialized in Italy. And systemic crisis might not bring about reform, but rather paralysis, breakdown, or something worse. After all, fascism was the "solution" to the crisis of post–World War I. The response of government to the euro zone crisis suggests that budget cutting will be seen as the answer to Italy's "problem," which does not augur well for population policy. There is a shrewd belief that individuals or families can find a way around social problems by playing the system to their own advantage. Government incapacity justifies "amoral familism." Because the effects of a pronatalist policy take decades to manifest themselves, pursuit of a long-term policy would require a vision and tenacity that Italian governments do not demonstrate.

Japan, unlike Italy, has pronatalist policies on the books, but they do not go far enough nor have they been applied in a determined and coherent way. Japan has a gridlocked political system and an ineffective state. Opposition to gender equality is strong; business resists reducing long working hours and eliminating other practices that force women to choose between family and career. And Japan's gigantic national debt, over 200 percent of gross national product, would seem to preclude costly long-term programs. Because Japan, unlike Italy, does not permit immigration, there is nothing to mitigate low birth rates in the short term. In that respect, Japan's situation is even worse than Italy's.

In the cases of Italy and Japan, there is a kind of pervasive fatalism about the inevitability of population decline and a lack of confidence in the ability of government to solve it. The immediacy of the crisis is blunted by the fact that these are still wealthy societies. As the Austrians used to say toward the end of their empire, the situation was "hopeless but not serious." Inaction will render it both hopeless and serious.

Singapore has sought to implement pronatalist policies but has not been successful. Singapore is quite different from Italy and Japan. It has not been hampered by the legacy of religion, fascism, and communism. Singapore's state apparatus is activist, and its single-party political system decisive and authoritarian. Singapore is an economic success story. What impedes the development of effective pronatalist policies is above all its commitment to free market capitalism and unwillingness to provide social services that could facilitate the reconciliation of the family and work. "Confucian values" are most likely merely a cover for minimizing social services. The government refuses to admit that its pronatalist policies have failed and has implicitly relied on immigration as a solution to its labor needs. Unfortunately, success in encouraging immigration has triggered an unprecedented angry response by citizens that brought about electoral humiliation for the People's Action Party in 2011. This defeat may eventually lead to a rethinking of the immigration option and perhaps renewed emphasis on pronatalism, but this has not yet happened.

The negative examples of Italy, Japan, and Singapore thus reinforce the contention that successful population policy requires significant allocation of financial resources to family policy, including social services, and support for women's need to reconcile work and children. This does not mean that all developed nations must replicate the postwar European welfare state, but it certainly does mean that successful population policy requires an activist state that assumes responsibility for the welfare of the family. Unfortunately, the tide is running against increased public support for families. *It is possible that developed nations with robust welfare states and high birth rates will become the exceptions, like islands in a sea of depopulation.* Globalization, growing inequality, and the dominance of the neoliberal model are all obstacles to raising fertility rates in developed societies.

Globalization brings down wages in developed societies to the level of developing societies. With globalization comes the decline of national economies, and consequently of the capacity of the state to play a planning role. Preoccupied with its very survival, the EU is in no condition today to play such a role either. With the rise of Asia, especially of China, fierce international competition threatens to eliminate jobs and dismember benefit programs in the high-wage, developed societies of Europe, Japan, and America.

With the decline of national economies, the interests of economic elites become dissociated from the nation. Foreign direct investment and offshoring enable them to make profits in other ways. Capital is mobile, whereas labor is much less so. Businesses based on imports and financial services can profit even when manufacturing declines. The result is the loss of high-skilled, semiprofessional, and professional employment and the proliferation of low-paying jobs, many of them part-time or temporary, mostly without social safety net protection and benefits. A two-tier system of employment often results, with insecure, underpaid jobs going to younger workers. As a result, they will be less likely to marry and have children. Eventually most jobs may become low-wage jobs.

Although globalization carries within it the potential for falling wages in developed societies, the trend toward income and wealth inequality is not a result of globalization alone. The end of the Cold War undermined the need for social solidarity in the West. Economic and political elites are now less willing to tolerate generous wage and benefit packages to maintain cohesion against the communist enemy. We are not "all in it together" anymore. In the United States, for instance, there has been a sharp rise in inequality. After the Great Depression, the concentration of wealth declined; the share of the top 1 percent fell from over one quarter of total wealth to about 10 percent, and the middle classes progressed upward. A distribution of wealth approximating that of 1929 has returned. Political power is becoming increasingly concentrated in the hands of the rich.[3] The return of very high levels of inequality contributes to low fertility.

One reason for relatively high U.S. birth rates, despite lack of social services for families, is the incredible optimism of most citizens. The American dream that each generation can do better than the last, the perception that economic opportunities are open to all, and belief in a dynamic labor market where high levels of unemployment are only temporary have fostered that optimism and with it a greater propensity to have children.

In the United States and Europe, there is now a strong sense that the rising middle class may be a thing of the past, that the Great Recession is not a mere bump in the business cycle but the portent of things to come, and that the next generations will face downward mobility and growing insecurity. These factors, in turn, will likely further reduce birth rates. In Europe, solutions to the euro crisis involve the adoption of "austerity" policies. Europeans fear that austerity will mean the end of many welfare state provisions that created peace, prosperity, and social security after the upheavals of the 1930s and World War II.

In nineteenth-century France, a nation where there was political equality but economic inequality, families invested all their resources in one or few children in order to achieve social mobility for the next generation. Today, where political equality continues in developed countries alongside rising economic inequality, families may adopt the French nineteenth-century strategy of investing in one or few children because they cannot afford more, and because by concentrating their resources on few children they hope to prevent their downward mobility.

Ironically, birth rates in China, the current beneficiary of globalization, are also low. The one-child policy is certainly the cause for the rapid decline of China's birth rate. But even if that policy is relaxed or eliminated, birth rates will probably remain low. Chinese families appear as determined as their nineteenth-century French counterparts to concentrate their resources in one child, preferably male, to improve his prospects for social mobility. China has not yet faced the downsides of its low birth rate, but it will. The state has dismantled many of the crude social welfare networks established during communism. As this generation of workers grows old, who will take care of them? With a predominance of male children (science has made it easy to choose the sex of one's children) what will happen to the Chinese family when today's male children seek mates? China will face the problem of growing old before it grows rich. Low birth rates may become pervasive in both the old developed nations facing decline and in developing nations on the rise.

Many states' responses to global economic recession seem to be influenced by neoliberal ideas. Cash-strapped countries facing growing entitlement costs may heed the notion that big government is the cause of the problem, rather than the solution. But before politicians begin to demolish the welfare state, they need to think twice. The last thing they should do is eliminate programs that encourage childbirth and family formation. To the extent that national leaders think long term, they should seek to improve the dependency ratio, that is, increase the percentage of the economically active versus non-active members of the population. They can do this by increasing birth rates and the percentage of women employed, because higher female employment coincides with higher birth rates where effective policies reconcile work and family. The precondition is the existence of serious political leadership that can plan for the long term and a financial situation that is stable enough so that investment in the future is still possible.

Any viable social welfare policy that promotes pronatalism must be founded on the basic principles developed by the Myrdals and cited earlier in this concluding chapter. Policies that would improve birth rates are high-quality public child care and generous maternity and paternity leave for all parents with return to employment guaranteed, regardless of whether parents have career-track jobs or "part-time" and fixed-term employment. Another priority area for action is higher education. Competitiveness today depends to a large extent on higher education, so it is in the national interest. At the same time, the rising cost of higher education in some countries has become the major expense for parents and determines whether they will have children, and, if so, how many. Student loan debt is another major factor in determining whether young, college-educated people will have children, and, if so, how many. Yet in many countries, the trend is to eliminate free higher education (the United Kingdom) or increase costs (the United States). Reversing this trend would improve the prospects for more competitive economies and higher birth rates.

The best argument against neoliberalism is that the economic and financial crisis we are now experiencing is not just a temporary economic downturn but a great secular trend, analogous to the 1930s, and that cutting budgets and awaiting the beneficial effects of the free market will not prove any more promising an approach now than in 1933. Prosperity is not just around the corner. Restoring economic and demographic growth will require an activist state. Because national economies have largely been superseded by globalization, greater international cooperation is required as well. Admittedly, the nation-state is saddled with most of the responsibilities for social welfare and education, yet it has reduced power over economic life. Even the European Union, which is much larger than a nation-state, has little control over the global economy.

Reversing the trend toward concentration of wealth and inequality and restoring faith in social mobility are pronatalist policies. In other words, just as in the 1930s, creating a sense of social security and optimism is necessary for economic and demographic revival. And as we have seen throughout this book, commitment to gender equality is also a sine qua non for pronatalism.

What if this does not happen? What if the developed nations choose to follow policies of retrenchment that lead to continued or accelerated fertility decline? What is the price of failure? The price will be paid in the exacerbation of the four national security threats outlined in the introduction

First, low birth rates combined with an aging population have a negative impact on the dependency ratio.[4] The enormous problem that this raises for the costs of retirement and health care are the best documented aspects of low fertility. The burden of entitlements grows to the point that they can hardly be supported; high national debt is often a symptom of the problem. Yet as the electorate ages, it becomes more and more difficult to contain these costs and increasingly likely that older voters will fight to preserve the benefits that accrue to the old at the expense of the young, which in the long term will only exacerbate the problem.[5] The danger is that the breakdown of the social welfare system will seem like a violation of the basic social contract established after the Great Depression and will exacerbate social tensions. That is already apparent in the immediate consequences of the Great Recession and the euro crisis; it could get a lot worse. The 1930s offers an example of how much worse it could get.

A second national security threat of low birth rates concerns economic growth and vitality. Although it is frequently asserted that the change in composition of societies occurring with an aging population and low fertility will lead to declining productivity and innovation, there has been remarkably little study of the full range of consequences. What happens to the life of society at a time of prolonged depopulation? What happens to the urban fabric, educational institutions, and social psychology? This is not wild speculation; some countries, including Japan, are actually losing population. Presumably, declining population will combine with other trends such as rural depopulation to produce a very different kind of political geography.

The third challenge of low birth rates to national security is changes in composition of the global population.[6] The prosperous, developed societies of Europe, America, and Asia are becoming a small minority in the world; that would be the case even if China was considered part of the developed world. In short, the rich "have" nations will constitute a diminishing percentage of the global population, whereas the most rapidly growing populations in Sub-Saharan Africa and the Middle East often lack the basic infrastructure of public-sector institutions, education, and technology necessary to sustain their growing populations. Many of the "have-nots" may become failed states before they go through the demographic transition and their fertility rates decline. The consequences, including regional and global conflict, could be the stuff of nightmares.

The fourth national security challenge created by low birth rates relates to immigration. Clearly, developed societies with low birth rates might benefit from immigration, and less developed societies, with huge excess population, would benefit from emigration. The problem is that the scale of respective needs would certainly differ. Places with very high birth rates and faltering economies might produce vast numbers of desperate people who want to emigrate, but developed societies will be unable or unwilling to accommodate them. In developed societies with low birth rates, immigration can serve as a supplement to a less-than-replacement birth rate (assuming successful assimilation policies), but not as an alternative. If the birth rate is the lowest low, the level of immigration would have to be extremely high to maintain population stability. Precisely because the birth rate of the children of immigrants falls to the level of the new country, these high levels of immigration would have to continue. It is hard to believe that any nation-state would voluntarily accept a flow of immigration so high that integration would no longer be possible. Indeed, opposition to immigration is being felt even in countries where immigration levels are now low. Immigration can fill in the needs of a society with a birth rate that is not at full replacement level; it cannot succeed in cases of lowest-low fertility. As stated above, population is not fungible. The danger of a large underclass of immigrants in a developed society who are defined as "other" is an obvious threat to social stability. The juxtaposition of lowest-low birth rates in some places and excessively high birth rates in others could result in great instability. The problem will only be solved if birth rates equalize all over the world at about replacement level, but, as we have seen, that will not happen without state intervention. Developed societies have a stake in providing support for birth control in potential crisis areas in the developing world (the United States has played an especially irresponsible role in this regard). They also need to raise their own low fertility.

It remains to be seen whether the political institutions by which men and women govern themselves and the return to increasingly unregulated free market capitalism are capable of meeting the challenges of declining birth rates. As we have seen, that challenge does not exist in isolation. It is intimately tied to the problem of globalization. Uncontrolled globalization could destroy the social welfare achievements of the developed world before they can be shared by the developing world. The population question is also closely related to climate change. Everything said about population in this work assumes the stability of a benign environment worldwide. Climate change could usher in a situation in which the successes of modern agriculture are rolled back and the world confronts a truly Malthusian crisis. It would exacerbate the twin dangers of overpopulation in some regions and population decline in others and lead to a world marked by instability, violence, crime, and interethnic tension.

Nations must promote a reasonable level of fertility before it becomes impossible to do so, that is, before they fall into Wolfgang Lutz's low fertility trap, described in the introduction. Lutz holds out some hope that prompt action in Central and Eastern Europe and the Mediterranean might reverse declining fertility before the self-reinforcing mechanism he describes kicks in, as he fears may already be the case in German-speaking Europe.[7] The need for effective pronatalist policies in developed societies is very real and delay may be fatal. Without action soon, a precipitous downward spiral may well ensue.

NOTES

Introduction

1. For an excellent, succinct account of the global demographic context today, see Jack Goldstone, "The New Population Bomb," *Foreign Affairs*, January–February 2010, 31–43.

2. See David S. Reher, "The Demographic Transition Revisited as a Global Process," *Population, Space and Place* 10 (2004): 25. In this article, Reher articulates a powerful revised version of the theory of the demographic transition.

3. Kingsley Davis, "Reproductive Institutions and the Pressure for Population" (1937), reprinted in *Population and Development Review* 23, no. 3 (September 1997): 616.

4. See, e.g., Ron Lesthaege, *The Unfolding Story of the Second Demographic Transition*, Report 10-696 (Ann Arbor: Population Studies Center, Institute for Social Research, University of Michigan, 2010); David S. Reher, "Towards Long-Term Population Decline: A Discussion of Relevant Issues," *European Journal of Population* 23, no. 2 (2007): 196.

5. Ronald E. Lee, "The Demographic Transition: Three Centuries of Fundamental Change," *Journal of Economic Perspectives* 17, no. 4 (Fall 2003): 167.

6. Christoph Conrad, Michael Lechner, and Welf Werner suggest this is the case for the former German Democratic Republic; Christoph Conrad, Michael Lechner, and Welf Werner, "East German Fertility after Unification: Crisis or Adaptation?" *Population and Development Review* 22, no. 2 (1996): 342.

7. On the current demographic crisis in Russia, see Nick Eberstadt, "The Dying Bear," *Foreign Affairs*, November–December 2011, 95–108.

8. According to the article "Strong Yen Is Dividing Generations in Japan," *New York Times*, August 2, 2012, Japanese politicians are tolerating a strong yen, which is undermining the manufacturing sector because of the

large population of retirees who benefit from the low prices of imported goods.

9. Goldstone, "New Population Bomb," 32–33.

10. Here is an example from a recent book: "What is certain is that national leaders cannot change the demographic future; they can only assess its ramifications upon the future security environment and prepare for it." Susan Yoshihara and Douglas A. Sylva, *Population Decline and the Remaking of Great Power Politics* (Washington, D.C.: Potomac Books, 2012), 8.

11. Wolfgang Lutz, Vegard Skirbekk, and Maria Rita Test, "The Low Fertility Trap Hypothesis: Forces That May Lead to Further Postponement and Fewer Births in Europe," International Institute for Applied Systems Analysis, Laxenburg, Austria, 2006, 13, www.oeaw.ac.at/vid/download/edrp _4_05.pdf. See also Wolfgang Lutz, "The Future of Human Reproduction: Will Birth Rates Recover or Continue to Fall?" *Ageing Horizons*, no. 7 (2007): 15–21.

12. Lutz, Skirbekk, and Test, "Low Fertility," 31.

Chapter One: Swedish Population Policy

1. Lena Sommestad, "Gender Equality: A Key to Our Future?" Swedish Institute, September 1, 2001, www.regeringen.se/pub/road/.../13/. This article came to my attention through Allan Carlson, "Sweden and the Failure of European Family Policy," *Society*, September–October 2005, 41–46.

2. Marques Childs, *Sweden: The Third Way* (New Haven, Conn.: Yale University Press, 1938).

3. Richard F. Tomasson, *Sweden: Prototype of Modern Society* (New York: Random House, 1970); Tomasson was a friend and colleague at the University of New Mexico.

4. Adolph Sturmthal, *The Tragedy of European Labour* (London: Victor Gollancz, 1944), 141.

5. Ibid., 142–43.

6. Walter Korpi, *The Working Class in Welfare Capitalism: Work, Unions and Politics in Sweden* (London: Routledge and Kegan Paul, 1978), 320–21.

7. Britta Hoem and Jan M. Hoem, "Sweden's Family Policies and Roller-Coaster Fertility," *Journal of Population Problems* 52, nos. 3–4 (1996): 2.

8. Allan Carlson, *The Swedish Experiment in Family Politics: The Myrdals and the Interwar Population Crisis* (New Brunswick, N.J.: Transaction,

1990), xi. For an excellent discussion of the role of the Myrdals in Swedish Social Democracy, see Tim Tilton, *The Political Theory of Swedish Social Democracy* (Oxford: Clarendon Press, 1990), 145–65.

9. Carlson, *Swedish Experiment*, 67.

10. Alva Myrdal, *Nation and Family: The Swedish Experiment in Democratic Family and Population Policy* (Cambridge, Mass.: MIT Press, 1968), 2.

11. Gunnar Myrdal, *Population: A Problem for Democracy* (Cambridge, Mass.: Harvard University Press, 1940).

12. Ibid., 103.

13. Ibid., 201.

14. Ibid., 207.

15. Gunnar Broberg and Mattias Tydén, "Eugenics in Sweden, Efficient Care," in *Eugenics and the Welfare State: Sterilization Policy in Denmark, Sweden, Norway and Finland*, edited by Gunnar Broberg and Nils Roll-Hansen (East Lansing: Michigan State University Press, 2005), 104.

16. Myrdal, *Population*, 216.

17. Ibid., 217.

18. Carlson, *Swedish Experiment*, 119.

19. Ibid., 176.

20. For a discussion of the respective roles of Gunnar and Alva, see Yvonne Hirdman, *Alva Myrdal: The Passionate Mind*, translated by Linda Schenk (Bloomington: Indiana University Press, 2008).

21. Statistics Sweden, *The Future Population of Sweden, 2009–2060* (Stockholm: Statistics Sweden, 2009), 17.

22. See Hoem and Hoem, "Sweden's Family Policies."

23. Jan M. Hoem, "Why Does Sweden Have Such High Fertility?" *Demographic Research* 13, no. 22 (2005): 570.

24. Peter McDonald, "The 'Toolbox' of Public Policies to Impact on Fertility: A Global View" (paper presented at the seminar "Low Fertility, Families, and Public Policy," European Observatory on Family Matters, Seville, September 15–16, 2000), https://digitalcollections.anu.edu.au/bitstream/1885/41446/3/sevilleMcD1.pdf.

25. Tommy Ferrarini and Anne-Zofie Duvander use the term "earner-carer" in *Conflicting Directions? Outcomes and New Orientations of Swedish Family Policy*, Working Paper 2010-4 (Stockholm: Stockholm University Linnaeus Center on Social Policy and Family Dynamics in Europe, 2010), 16, www.su.se/polopoly_fs/1.18703.1320939634!/WP_2010_4.pdf.

26. Swedish Ministry of Health and Social Affairs, "Financial Family Policy in Sweden," Stockholm, October 15, 2010, 3.

27. Helena Bergman and Barbara Hobson, "Compulsory Fatherhood: The Coding of Fatherhood in the Swedish Welfare State," in *Making Men into Fathers: Men, Masculinities and the Social Politics of Fatherhood,* edited by Barbara Hobson (Cambridge: Cambridge University Press, 2002), 115.

28. Rebecca Ray, Janet C. Gornick, and John Schmitt, "Parental Leave Policies in 21 Countries: Assessing Generosity and Gender Equality," Center for Economic and Policy Research, Washington, D.C., September 2008, revised June 2009, 15.

29. Paul Demeny, "Population Policy Dilemmas in Europe at the Dawn of the Twenty-First Century," *Population and Development Review* 29, no. 1 (March 2003): 22.

30. For a good account of Sweden's shift in housing policy, see Bengt Turner and Christine M. E. Whitehead, "Reducing Housing Subsidy: Swedish Housing Policy in an International Context," *Urban Studies* 39, no. 2 (2002): 201–17.

31. Ministry of Health and Social Affairs, "Financial Policy."

32. Ferrarini and Duvander, "Conflicting Directions," 18.

33. Bergman and Hobson, "Compulsory Fatherhood," 105.

34. Lena Sommestad, "Welfare State Attitude to the Male Breadwinner System: The United States and Sweden in Comparative Perspective," in *The Rise and Decline of the Male Breadwinner Family?* edited by Angélique Janssens (Cambridge: Cambridge University Press, 1998), 167.

35. Ibid., 169.

36. Bergman and Hobson, "Compulsory Fatherhood," 97.

37. Livia Sz. Olah and Eva M. Berhardt, "Sweden: Combining Child bearing and Gender Equality," *Demographic Research* 19, no. 28 (2008): 1114.

38. Peter McDonald, "Low Fertility and the State: The Efficacy of Policy," *Population and Development Review* 32 (September 2006): 489. See also Ulla Bjornberg, "Cohabitation and Marriage in Sweden: Does Family Form Matter?" *International Journal of Law, Policy, and the Family* 15, no. 3 (2001): 350–62.

39. Julia B. Isaacs, "A Comparative Perspective on Public Spending on Children," Brookings Center on Children and Families, Washington, D.C., November 2009, 13.

40. World Economic Forum, *The Global Competitiveness Report, 2010–2011* (Geneva: World Economic Forum, 2010), 15, 310–11.

41. Gunnar Andersson, *Childbearing Patterns of Foreign-Born Women in Sweden*, Working Paper 2001-011 (Rostock, Germany: Max Planck Institute for Demographic Research, 2001), 1.

42. McDonald, "Toolbox," 9–10.

43. McDonald, "Low Fertility," 495–96.

44. Demeny, "Population Policy," 23.

45. David Sven Reher, "Family Ties in Western Europe: Persistent Characteristics," *Population and Development Review* 24, no. 2 (1998): 203–34. In this significant and often-cited article, Reher distinguishes between the strong families of Mediterranean Europe and the weak families of the North. He demonstrates that their differences are based on long historical experience and are likely to endure.

Chapter Two: Demography in France

1. Jean-Claude Chesnais, "La politique de la population française depuis 1914," in *Histoire de la population française*, edited by Jacques Du Pâquier (Paris: Presses Universtitaires de la France, 1988), 4:185.

2. Institut nationale de la statistique et des études économiques, *Projections de population à l'horizon 2060*, Report 1320 (Paris: Institut nationale de la statistique et des études économiques, 2010), www.insee.fr/fr/themes/document.asp?ref_id=ip1320.

3. For an interesting comparison of Britain and France, see Jean-Claude Chesnais, "Révolution industrielle et révolution démographique au xviiie siècle: Le paradoxe France-Angleterre," in *La transition démographique* (Paris: Presses universitaires de la France, 1986), 309–29.

4. Jean-Pierre Bardet, "La chute de la fécondite," in *Histoire*, ed. Du Pâquier, 3:351.

5. Ibid., 377.

6. Ibid., 373.

7. Ibid., 369.

8. Yves Charbit, "La pensée démographique," in *Histoire*, ed. Du Pâquier, 3:475.

9. Émile Zola, *La fécondité* (Paris: Bibliothèque-Charpentier, 1907), 30.

10. This is not the place for a discussion of regional variations in birth rates nor of differences among social and religious groups. Thanks to the creation of the Institut National des Études Démographiques (INED), French demography has been studied in great detail. For our purposes, only basic trends are mentioned here.

11. Paul Leroy-Beaulieu, *La question de la population* (Paris: Félix Alcan, 1913), 220.

12. For the story of two commissions appointed to consider population issues before World War I and their meager accomplishments, see Alain Becchia, "Les milieux parlementaires et la dépopulation de 1900 à 1914," *Communications* 44 (1986): 201–46.

13. Richard Tomlinson, "The 'Disappearance' of France, 1896–1940: French Politics and the Birth Rate," *Historical Journal* 28, no. 2 (1985): 407.

14. Zola, *La fécondite*, 746.

15. Françoise Thébaud, "Les mouvement nataliste dans la France de l'entre deux-guerres: L'Alliance nationale pour l'accroissement de la population française," *Revue d'histoire moderne et contemporaine* 32, no. 2 (1985): 295.

16. Alphonse Landry, *La Révolution démographique* (Paris: INED, 1982; republished), 40.

17. Ibid., 53.

18. Ibid., 94–95.

19. Paul-André Rosental, *L'Intelligence démographique* (Paris: Jacob, 2003), 28.

20. Ibid., 19–20.

21. Ibid., 21.

22. Andrés Horacio Reggiani, "Procreating France: The Politics of Demography, 1919–1945," *French Historical Studies* 19, no. 3 (1996): 742.

23. Reggiani, "Procreating," 728.

24. *Journal Officiel de la République Française, Lois et Décrets*, July 30, 1939, 9607–27.

25. Rosental, *L'Intelligence*, 43.

26. Robert O. Paxton, *Vichy France: Old Guard and New Order, 1940–1944* (New York: W. W. Norton, 1975), 21.

27. Andrew Shennan, *Rethinking France: Plans for Renewal, 1940–1946* (Oxford: Clarendon Press, 1989), 207.

28. Rosental, *L'Intelligence*, 57.

29. Marie-Thérèse Letablier, "Fertility and Family Policies in France," *Journal of Population and Social Security (Population)* 1, supplement (2003): 245.

30. Claude Martin, "The Reframing of Family Policy," *Journal of European Social Policy* 20, no. 5 (2010): 412.

31. Ibid., 412.

32. Jean-Jacques Dupeyroux, Michel Borgetto, Robert Lafore, and Rolande Ruellan, *Droit de la sécurite sociale* (Paris: Dalloz, 2001), 691–92.

33. Kimberly Morgan, "The Politics of Mother's Employment: France in Comparative Perspective," *World Politics* 55, no. 2 (2003): 259.

34. Ibid., 260.

35. Ibid., 262.

36. Anne Reveillard, "Work/Family Policy in France: From State Familialism to State Feminism?" *International Journal of Law, Policy and the Family*, no. 20 (2006): 137–38.

37. Ibid., 137.

38. Morgan, "Politics," 282.

39. Reveillard, "Work/Family Policy," 142.

40. Laurent Toulemon, Ariane Pailhé, and Clémentine Rossier, "France: High and Stable Fertility," *Demographic Research* 19, no. 16 (2008): 533.

41. Because of the many differences between different national welfare policies, statistics are not perfectly comparable and are likely to only give a sense of order of magnitude.

42. Martin, "Reframing," 416.

43. Michel Chauvière, "Le rôle des lobbies dans la politique familiale," *Informations sociales* (CNAF), no. 157 (2010–11): 77.

44. Ibid., 74.

45. Martin, "Reframing," 416–17; Bertrand Fragonard (president of Haut conseil de la famille), interview by the author, Paris, March 15, 2011.

46. Olivier Thévenon, "Does Fertility Respond to Work and Family-Life Reconciliation Policy in France?" in *Fertility and Public Policy: How to Reverse the Trend of Declining Birth Rates*, edited by Noriyuki Takayama and Martin Werding (Cambridge, Mass.: MIT Press, 2009), 248.

47. Haut conseil de la famille, *Architecture de la politique familiale: Éléments de problèmatique*, adopted January 13, 2011, 4.

48. Ibid., 20.

49. Ibid., 8.

50. Ibid., 8–9.

51. Chauvière, "Rôle," 78n1.

52. Toulemon, Pailhé, and Rossier, "France: High and Stable," 525.

53. For an excellent history of changing French family policies, see Marc de Montalembert, "La politique familiale: Continuité et ruptures," *Cahiers français* 322 (September–October 2004): 65–70.

54. See Jacqueline Martin, "Politique familiale et travail des femmes mariées en France: perspective historique: 1942–1982," *Population* 53, no. 6 (November–December 1998): 1119–53.

55. Letablier, "Fertility," 246.

56. Thévenon, "Does Fertility Respond," 244.

57. Ibid., 243.

58. "La politique familiale: des 'retours sur l'investissement' qui dépendent des choix économiques et sociales" (working paper, Centre de recherche en économie de Sciences Po, Paris, September 2010), 5.

59. Jérôme Vignon, interview by the author, Paris, March 16, 2011.

60. Timothy Smith, *France in Crisis* (Cambridge: Cambridge University Press, 2004), 195.

61. Toulemon, Pailhé, and Rossier, "France: High and Stable," 534.

62. "La mise sous condition des ressources des allocations familiales: Une discrimination vraiment positive?" *Revue de droit sanitaire et social* 44, no. 2 (2008).

63. Ibid., 7.

64. Toulemon, Pailhé, and Rossier, "France: High and Stable," 503.

65. Bardet, "La chute de la fécondite," 362.

66. Toulemon, Pailhé, and Rossier, "France: High and Stable," 505.

67. Jean-Claude Chesnais, "La politique de population en France," in *Histoire des idées et politiques de population*, edited by Caselli Graziella, Vallin Jacques, and Wunsch Guillaume (Paris: INED, 2006), 7:799.

68. Toulemon, Pailhé, and Rossier, "France: High and Stable," 522.

Chapter Three: Italy

1. Manuela Naldini, *The Family in the Mediterranean Welfare States* (London: Frank Cass, 2003), 67.

2. Karl Marx, "The Critique of Hegel's Philosophy of Right," in *Karl Marx: Early Writings*, translated and edited by T. B. Bottomore (New York: McGraw Hill, 1964), 55.

3. Alessandra De Rose, Filomena Racioppi, and Anna Laura Zanata, "Italy: Delayed Adaptation of Social Institutions to Changes in Family Behaviour," *Demographic Research* 19 (2008): 665–704.

4. Peter McDonald, "The 'Toolbox' of Public Policies to Impact on Fertility: A Global View," paper presented at the seminar "Low Fertility, Families, and Public Policy," European Observatory on Family Matters, Seville, September 15–16, 2000, 2–4, https://digitalcollections.anu.edu.au/bitstream/1885/41446/.../sevilleMcD1.pdf.

5. Massimo Livi-Bacci, "Too Few Children, Too Much Family," *Daedulus*, Summer 2001, 142.

6. De Rose, Racioppi, and Zanata, "Italy: Delayed Adaptation," 691.

7. Julia B. Isaacs, *A Comparative Perspective on Public Spending on Children* (Washington, D.C.: Brookings Center on Children and Families, 2009), 13. But the elderly-child ratio is 5:2 in France!

8. Ibid., 13.

9. Edward Banfield, *The Moral Basis of a Backward Society* (New York: Free Press, 1985), 85.

10. Gianpiero Dalla Zuanna, "The Banquet of Aeolus: A Familistic Interpretation of Italy's Lowest Low Fertility," *Demographic Research* 4, no. 5 (2001): 141.

11. Ibid., 142.

12. David Sven Reher, "Family Ties in Western Europe: Persistent Characteristics," *Population and Development Review* 24, no. 2 (1998): 203–34.

13. Livi-Bacci, "Too Few Children," 148.

14. Dalla Zuanna, "Banquet," 151.

15. Ibid., 156.

16. Marco Simoni, "Labour and Welfare Reforms: The Short Life of Labour Unity," in *Italy Today: The Sick Man of Europe*, edited by Andrea Mammone and Giuseppe A. Veltri (London: Routledge, 2001), 237.

17. "Young, Smart and Fearing for the Future," *New York Times*, January 2, 2011.

18. John C. Caldwell and Thomas Schindlmayr, "Explanations of the Fertility Crisis in Modern Societies: A Search for Commonalities," *Population Studies* 57, no. 23 (2003): 250.

19. De Rose, Racioppi, and Zanata, "Italy: Delayed Adaptation," 671.

20. Ibid., 678.

21. See Carl Ipsen, "The Organization of Demographic Totalitarianism: Early Population Policy in Fascist Italy," *Social Science History* 17, no. 1 (1993): 71–108.

22. See Massimo Livi-Bacci, "Italy," in *Population Policy in Developed Countries*, edited by Bernard Berelson (New York: McGraw Hill, 1974), 657–58; and Naldini, *Family*, 67–74.

23. Naldini, *Family*, 69.

24. Chiara Saraceno with Manuela Naldini, *Mutamenti della famglia e politiche sociali in Italia* (Bologna: Il Mulino, 1998), 7.

25. Livi-Bacci, "Italy," 647.

26. Ibid., 659.

27. Saraceno, *Mutamenti*, 3.

28. Massimo Livi-Bacci, interview by the author, Rome, March 22, 2011.

29. Stefania Bernini, "Family Politics, the Catholic Church and the Transformation of Family Life in the Second Republic," in *Italy Today*, ed. Mammone and Veltri, 74.

30. Naldini, *Family*, 186.

31. Ibid., 187.

32. For a provocative anthropological point of view on the debate over assisted reproduction and pronatalism, see Elizabeth L. Krause and Milena Marchesi, "Fertility Politics as 'Social Viagra': Reproducing Boundaries, Social Cohesion, and Modernity in Italy," *American Anthropologist* 109, no. 2 (2007): 350–62.

33. Saraceno, *Mutamenti*, 184.

34. Ibid., 185.

35. For a very useful summary of the federalism debate, see Michael Keating and Alex Wilson, "Federalism and Decentralisation in Italy" (paper presented at Political Science Association conference, Edinburgh, March 29–April 1, 2010), www.psa.ac.uk/journals/pdf/5/2010/930_598.pdf.

36. Economist Intelligence Unit, *Country Report Italy*, April 2011, 6.

37. CIA, *The World Factbook,* 2013, https://www.cia.gov/library/publications/the-world-factbook/rankorder/21/2112rank.html.

38. Istituto Nazionale di Statistica, "Italy's Foreign Resident Population," September 29, 2011, http:/www.istat.it/en/archive40658.

39. Organization for Economic Cooperation and Development iLibrary, "Country Statistical Profile: Italy 2010," http://dx.doi.org/10.1787/20752288-2010-table-ita.

40. Francesca Bettio, Annamaria Simonazzi, and Paola Villa, "Change in Care Regimes and Female Migration: The Care Drain in the Mediterranean," *Journal of European Social Policy* 16, no. 3 (2006): 271–85.

Chapter Four: Japan

1. Mari Osawa, "Government Approaches to Gender Equality in the Mid-1990s," *Social Science Japan Journal* 3, no. 1 (2000): 18.

2. Florian Coulmas, *Population Decline and Aging in Japan: The Social Consequences* (New York: Routledge, 2007), 38.

3. National Institute of Population and Social Security Research, *Population Projections for Japan: 2001–2050* (Tokyo: National Institute of Population and Social Security Research, 2002). This projection is based on the middle variant (presupposing a slight increase in the TFR).

4. Ibid., 3.

5. Nicholas Eberstadt, "Japan Shrinks," *Wilson Quarterly*, Spring 2012, 30–31, www.wilsonquarterly.com/essays/japan-shrinks.

6. Peter McDonald, "The 'Toolbox' of Public Policies to Impact on Fertility: A Global View," paper presented at the seminar "Low Fertility, Families, and Public Policy," European Observatory on Family Matters, Seville, September 15–16, 2000, https://digitalcollections.anu.edu.au/bitstream/1885/41446/3/sevilleMcD1.pdf.

7. Leonard J. Schoppa, *Race for the Exits: The Unraveling of Japan's System of Social Protection* (Ithaca, N.Y.: Cornell University Press, 2006), 11.

8. Frances McCall Rosenbluth, "The Political Economy of Low Fertility," in *The Political Economy of Japan's Low Fertility*, edited by McCall Rosenbluth (Stanford, Calif.: Stanford University Press, 2007), 10.

9. Schoppa, *Race*, 65.

10. Patricia Boling, "Family Policy in Japan," *Journal of Social Policy* 27 (1998): 179.

11. Robert D. Retherford, Naohiro Ogawa, and Rikiya Matsukura, "Late Marriage and Less Marriage in Japan," *Population and Development Review* 27, no. 1 (2001): 65.

12. Ibid., 86–87.

13. Makoto Atoh, "Family Changes in the Context of Lowest-Low Fertility: The Case of Japan," *International Journal of Japanese Sociology*, no. 17 (2008): 18.

14. Coulmas, *Population Decline*, 43.

15. Retherford, Ogawa, and Matsukura, "Late Marriage," 91.

16. Chizuko Ueno, "The Declining Birthrate: Whose Problem?" *Review of Population and Social Policy* 7 (1998): 116.

17. Atoh, "Family Changes," 22. In Sweden in 1993, the average time spent by fathers was nine hours and five minutes per week.

18. Ueno, "Declining Birthrate," 118.

19. Retherford, Ogawa, and Matsukura, "Late Marriage," 91.

20. Shigeki Matsuda, "Japanese Young People's Marriage Intentions and the Growth in the Trend of Remaining Single," *Social Science Japan* 33 (2005): 5. For an interesting discussion of women and work in Japan, see Sylvia Ann Hewlett, Laura Sherbin, Catherine Fredman, Claire Ho, and Karen Sumberg, *Off-Ramps and On-Ramps Japan* (New York: Center for Work-Life Policy, 2011).

21. Retherford, Ogawa, and Matsukura, "Late Marriage," 89.

22. Coulmas, *Population Decline*, 59.

23. "Japan Population Decline: Third of Nation Have 'No Interest' in Sex," *Huffington Post*, January 30, 2012, www.huffingtonpost.com/2012/01/30/japan-population-decline-youth-no-sex_n_1242014.html; "Japanese Government: Young Men Losing Interest in Sex," Agence France Presse, January 14, 2011, www.rawstory.com/rs/2011/01/14/japanese-government-young-men-losing-interest-sex.

24. Coulmas, *Population Decline*, 58.

25. Mary C. Brinton, *Lost in Transition: Youth, Work and Instability in Postindustrial Japan* (New York: Cambridge University Press, 2011), 30–31.

26. Paul Wiseman, "No Sex Please—We're Japanese," *USA Today*, June 2, 2004.

27. Ronald R. Rindfuss, Minja Kim Choe, Larry L. Bumpass, and Noriko O. Tsuya, "Social Networks and Family Change in Japan," *American Sociological Review* 69, no. 6 (2004): 841.

28. Retherford, Ogawa, and Matsukura, "Late Marriage," 89.

29. Schoppa, *Race*, 60.

30. Ibid., 58.

31. Ibid., 59.

32. Toro Suzuki, "Lowest-Low Fertility and Governmental Actions in Japan," National Institute of Population and Social Security Research, Tokyo, 2006, 10, www.ier.hit-u.ac.jp/pie/stage1/Japanese/seminar/workshop 0612/suzuki.pdf.

33. Martin Fackler, "Career Women in Japan Find a Blocked Path," *New York Times*, August 6, 2007.

34. Robert D. Retherford and Naohiro Ogawa, *Japan's Baby Bust: Causes, Implications, and Policy Responses*, Working Paper 118 (Honolulu: East-West Center, 2005), 15.

35. Ibid., 17.

36. Boling, "Family Policy," 173.

37. Ibid., 175.

38. Toshihiko Hara, "Increasing Childlessness in Germany and Japan: Toward a Childless Society?" *International Journal of Japanese Sociology*, no. 17 (2008): 42.

39. Ogawa and colleagues state that the ideal family size in Japan remains about 2.5 children. Naohiro Ogawa, Robert D. Retherford, and Ribiya Matsukura, "Japan's Declining Fertility and Policy Responses," in *Ultra-Low Fertility in Pacific Asia: Trends, Causes and Policy Issues*, edited by Paulin Straughan, Angelique Chan, and Gavin Jones (London: Routledge, 2009), 46.

40. Leonard Schoppa, "Demographics and the State," in *The Demographic Challenge: A Handbook about Japan*, edited by Florian Coulmas, Harald Conrad, Annette Schad-Seifert, and Gabriele Vogt (Leiden: Brill, 2008), 648.

41. Patricia Boling, "Policies to Support Working Mothers and Children in Japan," in *The Political Economy of Japan's Low Fertility*, edited by Frances McCall Rosenbluth (Stanford, Calif.: Stanford University Press, 2007), 132.

42. Tuukka Toivonen, "Is Japanese Family Policy Turning 'Nordic'? Exposing Key Challenges for Japan's Parental Leave and Child Care Schemes" (Barnett Papers in Social Research, Department of Social Policy and Social Work, University of Oxford, 2007), 24.

43. Ibid., 22.

44. Ito Peng, "Social Care in Crisis: Gender, Demography, and Welfare State Restructuring in Japan," *Social Politics*, Fall 2002, 418.

45. Schoppa, *Race*, 159.

46. Ibid., 178.

47. Boling, "Family Policy," 186.

48. Mari Osawa, "Government Approaches to Gender Equality," 18. He refers to a specific government, but I think the comment has general application. For an extraordinary account of how the Japanese government is wasting $650 million to rebuild a sea wall that not only failed to prevent or alleviate the tsunami that also caused the Fukushima disaster but actually contributed to its ravages in the Kamaishi area, see Norimitsu Onishi, "Japan Revives a Sea Barrier That Failed to Hold," *New York Times*, November 3, 2011.

49. Makoto Atoh and Mayuko Akachi, "Low Fertility and Family Policy in Japan in an International Comparative Perspective" (discussion paper, Center for Intergenerational Studies, Institute of Economic Research, Hitotsubashi University, 2003), hermes-ir.lib.hit-u.ac.jp/rs/bitstream/10086/14372/1/pie_dp156.pdf.

50. Chico Harlan, "Japan Scales Back Child Subsidy Program," *Washington Post*, April 8, 2011.

51. Toivonen, "Is Japanese Family Policy Turning 'Nordic'?" 19.

52. Ibid., 2–3, on the DPJ as the opposition party.

53. Norihiro Kato, "Japan and the Ancient Art of Shrugging," *New York Times*, August 21, 2010.

Chapter Five: Singapore

1. Understanding population policy in Singapore is complicated by the fact that unlike the other case studies, Singapore is not a fully democratic polity. The PAP has no real opposition and thus acts as the government; the party announces policies and may or may not explain them. The Parliament does not provide a venue for debate that might force the government to further expound on the ideas underlying policies, evaluate methods, and assess policy failures. The traditionally cautious press is less so at present; however, the critical online journals do not provoke a reply from the government. My own experience as a scholar demonstrates that it is difficult to meet with decisionmakers. Thus, while it is easy to cite what government officials are saying, it is nearly impossible to determine what they are thinking.

2. David Drakakis-Smith, Elspeth Graham, Peggy Teo, and Ooi Giok Ling, "Singapore: Reversing the Demographic Transition to Meet Labour Needs," *Scottish Geographical Magazine* 109, no. 3 (1993): 152.

3. Shirley Hsiao-Li Sun, *Population Policy and Reproduction in Singapore: Making Future Citizens* (London: Routledge, 2012), 68.

4. Geraldine Heng and Janadas Devan, "State Fatherhood: The Politics of Nationalism, Sexuality and Race in Singapore," in *Bewitching Women, Pious Men: Gender and Politics in Southeast Asia*, edited by Aihwa Ong and Michael G. Peletz (Berkeley: University of California Press, 1995), 196.

5. Elspeth Graham, "Singapore in the 1990s: Can Population Policies Reverse the Demographic Transition?" *Applied Geography* 15, no. 3 (1995): 221.

6. Drakakis-Smith et al., "Singapore Reversing," 152.

7. David Drakakis-Smith and Elspeth Graham, "Shaping the Nation-State: Ethnicity, Class, and the New Population Policy in Singapore," *International Journal of Population Geography* 2 (1996): 71.

8. As Heng and Devan put it, "The institution of what can be called, for suggestive convenience, an 'internalized Orientalism' makes available to *postcolonial* authority the knowledge power that *colonial* authority wielded over the local population, and permits, in Singapore, an overwhelmingly Western-educated political elite to dictate the qualities that would constitute Chineseness." Heng and Devan, "State Fatherhood," 207.

9. Diane K. Mauzy and R. S. Milne, *Singapore: Politics under the People's Action Party* (London: Routledge, 2002), 57.

10. Ibid., 52.

11. National Population and Talent Division, *Population in Brief 2010* (Singapore: Government of Singapore, 2010), www, www.nptd.gov.sg/content/NPTD/news/_jcr_content/par_content/download_31/file.res/Population%20in%20Brief%202010.pdf.

12. Gavin W. Jones, "Population Policy in a Prosperous City-State: Dilemmas for Singapore," *Population and Development Review* 38, no. 2 (2012): 319. Jones points out (p. 316) that although Singapore's birth rates are low for a nation, they are above birth rates in many Asian cities. But that does not help Singapore—although arguably a city, it functions as an independent state.

13. Ibid., 320.

14. Saw Swee-Hock, *Population Policies and Programmes in Singapore* (Singapore: Institute of South Asian Studies, 2005), 115.

15. Graham, "Singapore in the 1990s," 221.

16. Saw Swee-Hock, *Population Policies*, 59. This book is the source for much of my information on government programs, which in several cases I have paraphrased.

17. Vivienne Wee, "Children, Population Policy, and the State in Singapore," in *Children and the Politics of Culture*, edited by S. Stevens (Princeton, N.J.: Princeton University Press, 1995), 195–96.

18. Ibid., 199.

19. Ibid., 203.

20. Heng and Devan, "State Fatherhood," 198. These authors provide a fascinating discussion of the "great marriage debate," which includes Lee Kuan Yew's nostalgic references to polygamy.

21. Saw Swee-Hock, *Population Policies*, 162.

22. Graham, "Singapore in the 1990s," 230–31.

23. K. K. Choo, "The Shaping of Childcare and Preschool Education in Singapore: From Separatism to Collaboration," *International Journal of Child Care and Education Policy* 4, no. 2 (2010): 23–24.

24. Singapore Department of Statistics, *Population Trends* (Singapore: Singapore Department of Statistical, 2010).

25. Sun, *Population Policy*, 97.

26. Shirley Hsiao-Li Sun, "Re-Producing Citizens: Gender, Employment and Work–Family Balance Policies in Singapore," *Journal of Workplace Rights* 14, no. 3 (2009): 351.

27. Sun, *Population Policy*, 99.

28. Shirley Hsiao-Li Sun, "From Citizen-Duty to State Responsibility: Globalization and Nationhood in Singapore," *New Global Studies* 4, no. 3 (2010): 20–21.

29. Ibid., 22.

30. Shirley Hsiao-Li Sun, "Decision Makers' Framing, Knowledge and Perceptions: Social Class and Pronatalist Population Policies in Singapore," *Social & Public Policy Review* 6, no. 2 (2012): 40–66, http://works.bepress.com/shirleysun/8.

31. Ibid., 31.

32. Ibid., 30.

33. Ibid., 38.

34. Peter McDonald, "Gender Equity, Social Institutions and the Future of Fertility," *Journal of Population Research* 17, no. 1 (2000): 9.

35. Elspeth Graham, Peggy Teo, Brenda S. A. Yeoh, and Susan Levy, "Reproducing the Asian Family across the Generations: 'Tradition,' Gender and Expectations in Singapore," *Asia-Pacific Population Journal* 17, no. 2 (2002): 61–86.

36. Paulin Tay Straughan, Angelique Chan, and Gavin Jones, "From Population Control to Fertility Promotion: A Case Study of Family Policies and Fertility Trends in Singapore," in *Ultra-Low Fertility in Pacific Asia: Trends, Causes and Policy Dilemmas*, edited by Gavin Jones, Paulin Tay Straughan, and Angelique Chan (London: Routledge, 2009), 186.

37. Saw Swee-Hock, *The Population of Singapore*, 2nd ed. (Singapore: Institute of Southeast Asian Studies, 2007), 253.

38. Cited by Liu Hong, "Transnational Chinese Social Sphere in Singapore: Dynamics, Transformations and Characteristics," *Journal of Current Chinese Affairs* 41, no. 2 (2012): 37–60.

39. Mah Bow Tan (minister of national development), "Why We Need 6.5 Million People," *Petir*, March–April 2010, www.pap.org.sg/articleview .php?folder=PT&id=1758.

40. Brenda S. A. Yeoh and Weiqiang Lin, "Rapid Growth in Singapore's Immigration Population Brings Policy Challenges," *Migration Information Source*, Singapore, April 2012, www.migrationinformation.org/feature/ display.cfm?ID=887.

41. Liu Hong, "Transnational Chinese Social Sphere."

42. Yeoh and Lin, "Rapid Growth," 5.

43. "Singapore's Election: A Win-Win Election?" *Economist*, May 8, 2011.

44. *Temasek Review Emeritus*, December 31, 2010. The blog has been renamed *TR Emeritus* and can be found at www.tremeritus.com.

45. Jeremy Grant, "Olympic Medal Stokes Debate on Singapore Immigration," *Financial Times*, August 10, 2012.

46. Yap Mui Teng, Kang Soon Hock, and Chua Chun Ser, "Scenarios of Future Population Growth and Change in Singapore," *IPS Update* (Institute of Policy Studies, Singapore), March 2011.

47. Tommy Koh, "What Singapore Can Learn from Europe," *Straits Times*, May 19, 2012.

48. Maru Bhaskaran, Ho Seng Chee, Donald Low, Tan Kim Song, Sudhir Vadaketh, and Yeoh Lam Keong, "Background Paper: Inequality and the Need for a New Social Compact," in *Singapore Perspectives 2012* (Singapore: Institute for Policy Studies of the Lee Kuan Yew School of Public Policy, 2012), 16.

49. Ibid., 18.

50. Ibid., 22.

Conclusion

1. Of course, we have seen that the first steps in this direction took place in the last months of the Third Republic, as the threat of war focused the minds of the political elite. The Family Code marked an important step in providing significant financial support for families—prefiguring the welfare state. Conversely, there was no recognition of the linkage between low birth rates and the generalized lethargy of French society.

2. The best account of this issue remains that given by Karl Polanyi, *Origins of Our Time: The Great Transformation* (London: Gollancz, 1946).

3. See George Packer, "The Broken Contract," *Foreign Affairs* 90, no. 6 (2011).

4. For a recent discussion of the impact of population decline, written from a somewhat more optimistic point of view, see David Coleman and Robert Rowthorn, "Who's Afraid of Decline? A Critical Examination of Its Consequences," *Population and Development Review* 37, supplement (2011): 217–48. The best general article on the future of population is by David S. Reher, "Towards Long-Term Population Decline: A Discussion of Relevant Issues," *European Journal of Population* 23, no. 2 (2007): 189–207.

5. For a thoughtful discussion of this topic, see Peter Peterson, "The Global Aging Crisis," *Foreign Affairs* 78, no. 1 (1999).

6. See Pierre Buhler, "Puissance et démographie: La nouvelle donne," *l'Annuaire Français des Relations Internationales* (Brussels: Éditions Bruylant, 2004).

7. Wolfgang Lutz, Vegard Skirbekk, and Maria Rita Test, "The Low Fertility Trap Hypothesis: Forces That May Lead to Further Postponement and Fewer Births in Europe," International Institute for Applied Systems Analysis, Laxenburg, Austria, 2006, 13, www.oeaw.ac.at/vid/download/edrp_4_05.pdf.

Eberstadt, Nicholas, 90
école maternelle (France), 61
economic growth, 143
Economist: on Italy's economic problems, 87; on Singapore's immigration policy, 127
education: and competitiveness, 141; in France, 48, 59; in Italy, 72; in Japan, 96, 102; in Singapore, 112, 113, 115, 117–18; in Sweden, 31. *See also* early childhood education; preschool
Elbaum, Mireille, 66
elderly-child spending ratio, 36, 73, 107
elections, 112–13, 127
Equal Opportunities Employment Law of 1985 (Japan), 105
Esposito, Francesca, 76
ethnic groups in Singapore, 114
eugenics, 11, 117–20, 126
euro crisis, 87–88, 136, 140, 143
Europe and European Union: birth rates in, 1; demographic transition in, 3; and federalism, 86; and globalization, 142; immigration within, 9; labor migration in, 38; middle class in, 140; pronatalism in, 6. *See also specific countries*
extramarital births. *See* nonmarital births

families and familialism: and Catholic Church, 11–12, 58–59, 135; in France, 43, 47, 56, 58–59, 63–64; and gender equality, 2; in Italy, 64, 73–77; role of, 3; in Sweden's population policy, 34–36, 64. *See also* "traditional family"
family allowances, 72, 78, 79, 104
Family Code of 1939 (France), 52, 53, 54, 164n1
Family Planning Association (Singapore), 116

fascism: Italy's population policy impacted by, 78–80; and pronatalist policies, 4–5, 11
La fécondité (Zola), 49
federalism, 86–87
feminism, 21, 27, 57, 85
Ferry Laws (France), 59
fertility within marriage: in Japan, 93, 100–103; in Singapore, 115. *See also* birth rates
finances: for France's population policy, 60–61, 71; Italy's economic and financial problems, 87–89, 136; for Sweden's population policy, 36–37, 71
fiscal federalism, 86
flexible contract employment, 72
flex time, 120, 121, 123
Fragonard, Bertrand, 61
France, 18, 42–69; birth rate trends in, 3, 4, 44–46; contemporary population policy in, 60–67; demographic transition in, 44–46; funding of population policy in, 60–61, 71; history of population policy in, 44–60; immigration to, 8; political environment in, 51; post–World War II population policy in, 54–60; pronatalism in, 5, 46–54; success of population policy in, 68–69, 131
France in Crisis (Smith), 66
Franco-Prussian War (1870–71), 42, 43
Fukushima nuclear disaster (2011), 91, 109

gay rights, 99–100
gender equality: in France, 56–57, 63; in Japan, 92, 137; in Singapore, 125; in Sweden, 21, 27–28, 29, 30, 34; trends in, 2
Germany: demographic transition in, 3; fascism's impact on population policy in, 5, 11; number of children desired by parents in, 16;